CYPRUS

Travel with Marco Polo Insider Tips

INSIDER TIP
Your shortcut to a great experience

MARCO POLO TOP HIGHLIGHTS

PÁFOS MOSAICS ★1

The Roman tilers of Cyprus really did have their work cut out here. Many of the villas in this archaeological park boast beautiful patterned floors made from colourful small tiles.

Tip: Get your selfie stick out in order to capture an entire mosaic in one picture.

➤ p. 84, Páfos

KÝKKO MONASTERY ★2

Cyprus's oldest monastery is proof (if it were needed) that bling is nothing new. There is gold dripping from every corner. And all of that at an altitude of 1,200m.

Tip: If you want to bring out the colour of the ornate gemstones and jewels among the gold, be careful to get the lighting right.

➤ p. 105, Tróodos

PÁNO LÉFKARA ★3

The fine embroidery produced in this small village has become world famous and – for the keen investor – quite valuable.

Tip: For best results, take photos of the women sewing at eye level (ask permission first).

➤ p. 53, Lárnaka

İNCIRLI CAVE ★4

Climbing up mountains is one thing but climbing into them gives you a whole different perspective. The island's biggest caves contain staggering rock formations.

➤ p. 117, Northern Cyprus

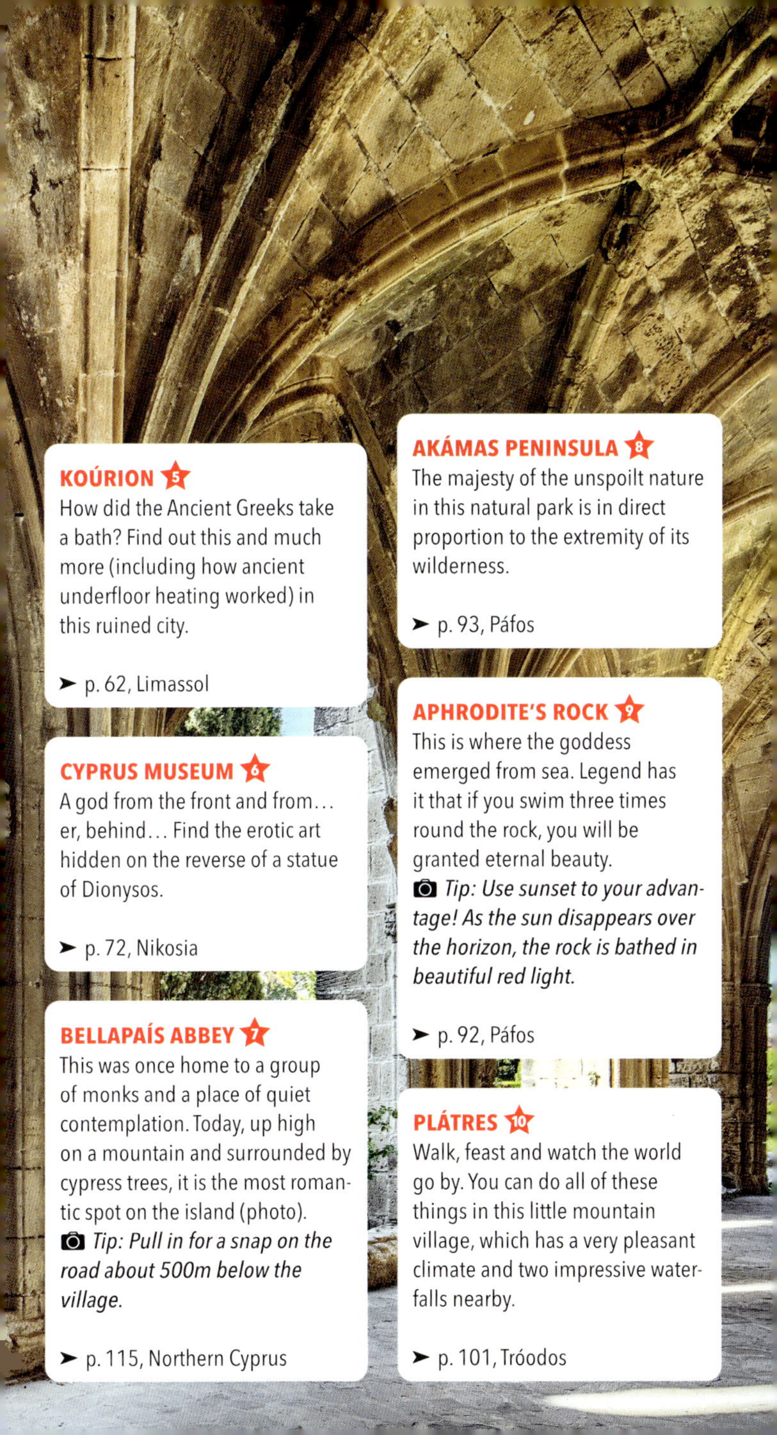

KOÚRION 5

How did the Ancient Greeks take a bath? Find out this and much more (including how ancient underfloor heating worked) in this ruined city.

➤ p. 62, Limassol

CYPRUS MUSEUM 6

A god from the front and from… er, behind… Find the erotic art hidden on the reverse of a statue of Dionysos.

➤ p. 72, Nikosia

BELLAPAÍS ABBEY 7

This was once home to a group of monks and a place of quiet contemplation. Today, up high on a mountain and surrounded by cypress trees, it is the most romantic spot on the island (photo).

Tip: Pull in for a snap on the road about 500m below the village.

➤ p. 115, Northern Cyprus

AKÁMAS PENINSULA 8

The majesty of the unspoilt nature in this natural park is in direct proportion to the extremity of its wilderness.

➤ p. 93, Páfos

APHRODITE'S ROCK 9

This is where the goddess emerged from sea. Legend has it that if you swim three times round the rock, you will be granted eternal beauty.

Tip: Use sunset to your advantage! As the sun disappears over the horizon, the rock is bathed in beautiful red light.

➤ p. 92, Páfos

PLÁTRES 10

Walk, feast and watch the world go by. You can do all of these things in this little mountain village, which has a very pleasant climate and two impressive waterfalls nearby.

➤ p. 101, Tróodos

CONTENTS

NORTHERN CYPRUS
NICOSIA
TRÓODOS
AGÍA NÁPA & LÁRNAKA
PÁFOS
LIMASSOL

CONTENTS

⏲	Plan your visit	🍴	Eating/drinking	☂	Rainy day activities
€–€€€	Price categories	🧺	Shopping	🐷	Budget activities
(*)	Premium-rate phone number	🍸	Going out	👧	Family activities
		⛱	Top beaches	⚑	Classic experiences

(🕮 A2) Refers to the removable pull-out map
(🕮 a2) Refers to the additional map on the pull-out map
(0) Located off the map

BEST OF CYPRUS

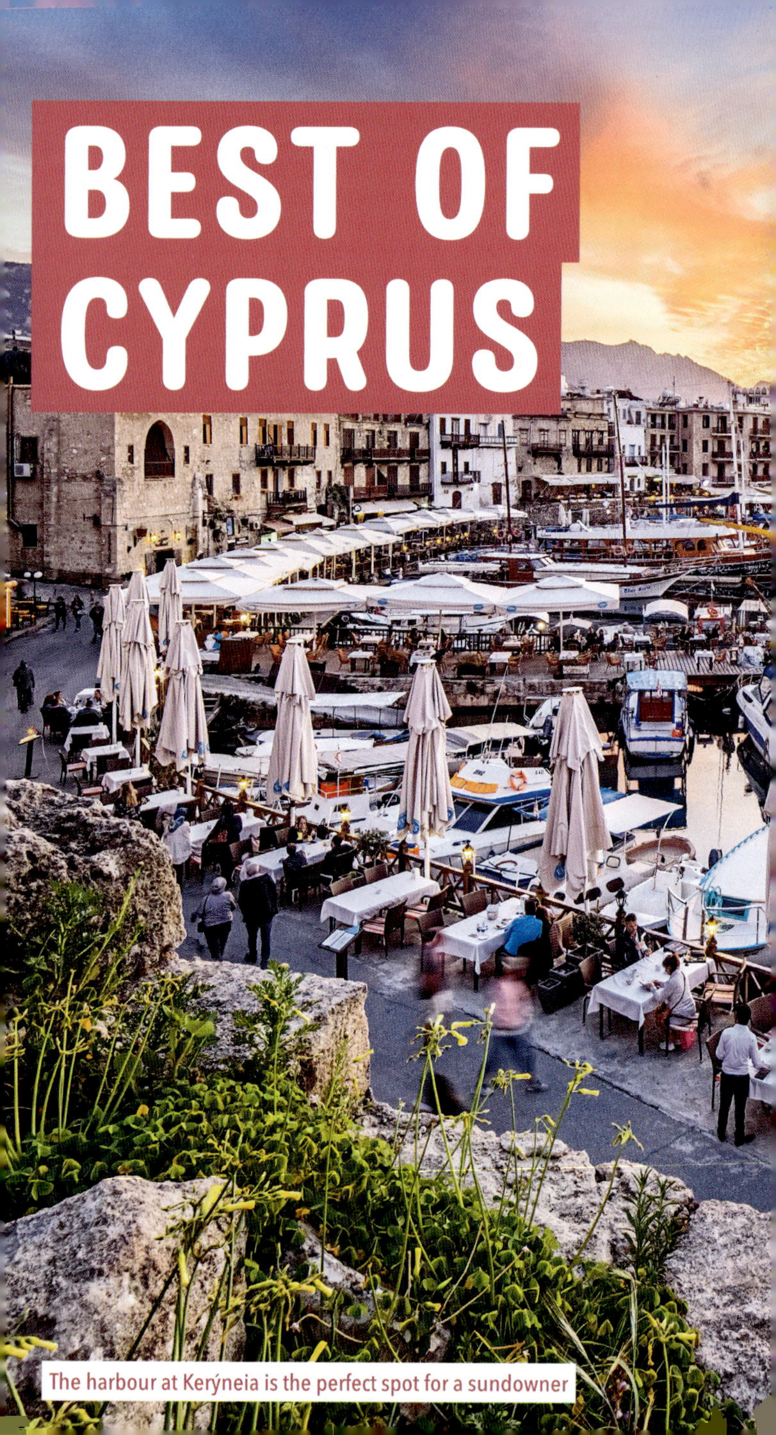

The harbour at Kerýneia is the perfect spot for a sundowner

HOTEL BRITISH
WHITE PEARL HOTEL
BIG BOSS
VIP

BEST WHEN IT RAINS

ACTIVITIES TO BRIGHTEN YOUR DAY

MODEL FOR AN ARTIST

Theo Michael in Lárnaka has a unique style that is reminiscent of old film posters. In his large studio, he'll draw or paint your portrait, in pencil or in oils, large or small.

➤ p. 50, Agía Nápa & Lárnaka

THE PLEASURE OF WINE

If you spend enough time learning about the development of Cypriot wine and the industry around it, you may well find yourself desperate for a glass. And thankfully the *Cyprus Wine Museum* in Erími allows you do both in one place. If you don't make it there, there are plenty of opportunities to take part in (usually) free tastings on Cyprus's seven wine routes (most of which are in Tróodos).

➤ p. 62, Limassol, p. 106, Tróodos

RELAX IN A STEAMY BATH

Use the bad weather to revive your tired muscles in the steamy comfort of the restored Ottoman *Omeriye steam baths*. The hot water and will make you feel as good as new.

➤ p. 77, Nicosia

INDOOR SHOPPING

Enjoy browsing in the old market halls, where groceries are on sale along with souvenirs and clothing. The *Market Hall of Páfos* was refurbished for the city's time as European Capital of Culture 2017.

➤ Páfos, p. 89

ADMIRE THE GOLD TREASURE

There's no better way to spend a rainy day than at the house of the person responsible for the weather, and in these parts that's the Virgin Mary; and she is worshipped at *Kýkko Monastery* (photo). Thanks to the many beneficiaries, there are plenty of gold objects and other treasures to admire.

➤ p. 105, Tróodos

BEST ON A BUDGET

FOR SMALLER WALLETS

FREE WIFI FOR EVERYONE

Although some providers have reintroduced roaming charges for UK visitors, you still don't need to use much data on Cyprus. Among other places, the *city beaches in Páfos* (Bania and SODAP beach) and *Agía Nápa* offer *free WiFi*.

➤ p. 44, Agía Nápa, p. 90, Páfos

SHOOTING STARS

A starscape worthy of the world's greatest artists. The best view is from one of the island's more remote beaches, or in the Tróodos mountains. In Lárnaka, on the *Finikoudes promenade*, a man offers his telescope for stargazing for just 2 euros. August is the ideal time as you can watch the meteor shower of shooting stars.

➤ p. 49, Agía Nápa & Lárnaka

PARK & RIDE

The traffic in Limassol is a nightmare for visitors. Save yourself the stress and expensive parking fees and park your car *free of charge at the zoo* and then take a *bus downtown*.

➤ p. 58, Limassol

TRY SOME!

In *Anógyra*, guests with inquiring minds are particularly welcome. If you have always wanted to know how carob sweets *pasteli* (photo) or squeaky halloumi cheese is made, you can watch the producers here free of charge and taste the fresh produce.

➤ p. 63, Limassol

CULTURAL CAPITALISM

A bank building where – for once – something other than finance is the centre of attention. The *Bank of Cyprus Cultural Foundation* in Nicosia's Old Town has an amazing collection. Stroll through thousands of years of Cypriot art history without having to pay a penny for the privilege.

➤ p. 68, Nicosia

BEST WITH CHILDREN

FUN FOR YOUNG & OLD

MAKE A SPLASH

Waterworld, Cyprus's biggest water park, has 150m-long slides and wave machines which can create breakers over 1m high. For more sedate fun, the whole family can navigate the "Odysseus River" in a dinghy.

➤ p. 43, Agía Nápa & Lárnaka

BACK TO NATURE

Kids can explore the unique biodiversity of the Akrotíri Peninsula, as well the natural and cultural history of Cyprus, at the *Akrotíri Environmental Education Centre*. Discover the mini-hippos and dwarf elephants that roamed the island thousands of years ago, learn to weave a basket and, coming back to the present, spot storks and flamingos from the centre's terrace.

➤ p. 63, Limassol

DOWN ON THE FARM

Where do milk, cheese and eggs come from? *Riverland Bio Farm* has the answers to these and many other questions. There are also opportunities to pet and stroke the animals, and to take part in activities from horse riding to archery and kayaking.

➤ p. 78, Nicosia

TURTLE BABIES

Lie in wait with your little ones trying to catch a glimpse of turtles laying their eggs. Or – perhaps even better – be there when the hatchlings make their first foray from the conservation station in Alagadi down to the sea.

➤ p. 117, Northern Cyprus

BLOWING BUBBLES

In many of Cyprus's dive centres, children over eight years old can take a PADI-certified *Bubblemaker* scuba-diving course. With all the necessary equipment available, good swimmers can safely experience the underwater world in the nearby shallow seas.

➤ p.120, Northern Cyprus

BEST

CLASSIC EXPERIENCES

ONLY ON CYPRUS

ALL YOU CAN EAT

It is often said that Cypriots eat as though there were no tomorrow. In *Nápa*, a traditional taverna in Agía Nápa, you can experience first hand how a true Cypriot dinner requires at least 15 different dishes on the table: from salads and tzatziki to calamari and lamb cutlets.

➤ p. 43, Agía Nápa & Lárnaka

A BEER IN THE BORDER ZONE

One of the very few villages on Cyprus where Greek and Turkish Cypriots still live together is *Pýla*, near Lárnaka. In the village square of this no man's land between north and south you have the choice between Greek-Cypriot and Turkish beer and can chat to the UN soldiers who hang around here.

➤ p. 51, Agía Nápa & Lárnaka

VILLAGE FOLK DANCING

If you want to experience true Cypriot tradition, make sure you visit *Pissoúri*. In the summer, the O'Vrakas and Symposio taverna owners organise *folklore evenings* (photo) around the village square.

➤ p. 63, Limassol

FRESH SPRING WATER

On hot days, nothing tastes better than a glass of water. At the *burbling springs in the Tróodos mountains*, many Cypriots collect supplies of clear mountain water to last for several weeks here. If you're hiking in the area, feel free to fill some empty bottles at the sparkling spring.

➤ p. 103, Tróodos

PICNIC IN THE FOREST

At the weekend "do as the Cypriots do" and pack everything you need for a delicious meal or barbecue and head to one of the many picnic sites in the north or south of the island.

➤ p. 106

GET TO KNOW CYPRUS

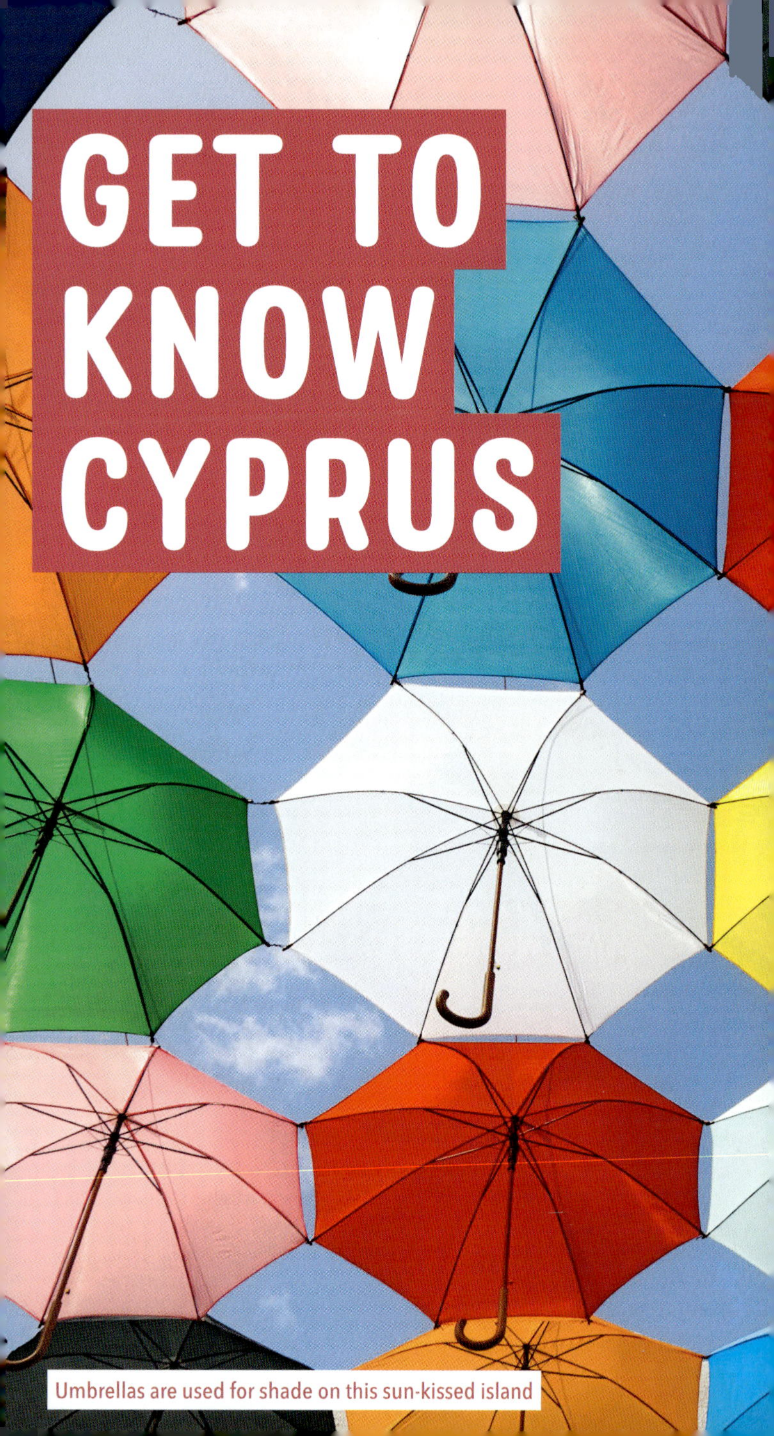

Umbrellas are used for shade on this sun-kissed island

DISCOVER CYPRUS

Find the real Cyprus in villages such as Pedoulás in the Tróodos mountains

It seems fitting that Aphrodite, the goddess of beauty and love, should hail from Cyprus. This sunny island in the easternmost corner of the Mediterranean is the ideal home for a beauty expert, thanks to its long, dreamy beaches, crystal-clear waters, wild cliffs and striking mountains.

HISTORY EVERYWHERE YOU LOOK

There are times when the presence of history in Cyprus becomes overwhelming, and it begins to feels almost like a theme park. Traces of settlers from every period of history remain: Crusaders' castles, Byzantine monasteries, Gothic cathedrals and Turkish mosques. But the past has also left a visible scar right across the island in the form of a border that, since 1974, has divided Cyprus into

7000–1050 BCE Cyprus is settled by people from Anatolia

294 BCE–391 CE Becomes a province of the Egyptian Ptolemaic Empire, which becomes part of the Roman Empire from 58 BCE

391–1191 CE Cyprus belongs to the Eastern Roman Empire, later to the Byzantine Empire

1191–1489 The Franks govern Cyprus

1489–1571 The island belongs to Venice until the Ottoman Empire conquers it in 1571

1878–1925 British rule

north and south. That said, as a tourist you will only truly realise the trauma of this division if you spend time on the border itself or talk to Cypriots about their experiences.

THE BUZZ OF A CAPITAL CUT THROUGH BY A BORDER

Nicosia's historic old town is the main magnet for visitors to Cyprus's capital. To reach it, most people go through the central Eleftheria Square (locals refer to it as the "frying pan" thanks to its gleaming white concrete). It marks the entrance to Lidras Street, a pedestrianised parade of cafés, shops and bars. However, after about 600m, this normality comes to an abrupt end as you encounter a Greek-Cypriot border post. To continue, you have to cross a thin buffer zone patrolled by UN soldiers, before showing your passport on the Turkish-Cypriot side and re-entering normality. On this side everything seems to be more or less exactly the same, but also a little bit different – the locals here are Muslims rather than Christians and they speak Turkish instead of Greek. That said, they also like to sit in cafés and play the same dice game, even if they call it it *távli*, while the others say *tavla*.

CITIES AND COASTAL TOWNS

In the three large cities on the southern coast – Limassol, Lárnaka and Páfos – you won't notice the division at all. They are modern metropolitan cities. English is spoken in the hotels, restaurants and shops. Menus and signposts are bilingual. The majority of the island's coastal towns are very much geared up for tourism

1960 Cyprus gains independence; civil war begins

1974 Turkish invasion after a coup staged by the Greek military junta; the island is divided

1983 Unilateral proclamation of the "Turkish Republic of Northern Cyprus"

2004 Southern Cyprus joins the EU

2020 The ghost town of Varósha partially reopens after 46 years

2022 A ban on plastic disposable packaging comes into force and extremely welcoming to passing travellers. The island is united in being a superb place to spend a peaceful holiday on the Mediterranean.

COOL SUMMITS AND SUNNY WINE

On the small island of Cyprus there are two mountain ranges. In the north, the Kerýneia mountains tower over the coast and its towns and villages. The dramatic Tróodos mountain range in the south is most famous for the 1,951m-high summit of Mount Ólympos; its altitude and thick forests make it a cool oasis even at the height of summer. Fruit and nut trees grow in the valleys, while vines are cultivated on the slopes. Several vineyards in the Tróodos mountains produce fine wines that are prized by those in the know; they can be tasted at wineries along the island's seven wine routes. While three Crusaders' fortresses attract visitors to the Kerýneia range, the Tróodos mountains are jam-packed with monasteries and characteristic barn-roofed churches with their colourful wall paintings; ten are listed as UNESCO World Heritage Sites.

INSIDER TIP
Mountain tipples

TAKE IT SLOW

Cypriots live by the motto "sigá, sigá", in Greek, or "yavaş, yavaş", in Turkish. In English, it means "slowly, slowly", and you will see evidence of this attitude if you take an evening stroll through the old parts of town, where the owners of dusty shops move at glacial pace.

PEACE, PARAGLIDING AND PARTYING

Cyprus's coast is ideal for swimming. Sandy beaches stretch for miles along the east coast and on the south coast around Lárnaka; there are multiple sandy coves around Agía Nápa, Limassol, Páfos and Kerýneia, and you'll find pebbly beaches at Pólis. Cyprus is a sporty destination: kitesurfers sail through the air; divers descend to sea caves and shipwrecks, while hiking trails, mountain bike routes and riding stables will keep you active on dry land. At night, Agía Nápa is considered the clubbing mecca of the eastern Mediterranean, while the beach clubs of Lárnaka and Limassol are well-known party hubs.

IN THE FOOTSTEPS OF A GODDESS

Aphrodite, though, preferred the quiet, calm places on her home island of Cyprus. Far from the beach of Pétra tou Romíou, where she emerged from the waves, and from Páfos, the location of her most important sanctuary, she met her lover Adonis for a romantic date in a small spring pool at what is today Pólis. To sit here on a restaurant terrace, enjoying fresh fish and a glass of Cypriot wine, looking over the wide bay and out to sea, will transport even the most stressed traveller into the calm, serene world that Cypriots aspire to.

AT A GLANCE

1,155,000
population
Birmingham: 1,153,717

8,000
couples travel to Cyprus every year to get married

782km
coastline
Welsh coast: 1,400km

9,251 km²
area
Six times bigger than London

HIGHEST MOUNTAIN: Ólympos
1,951m
Unfortunately, the summit is closed to visitors

WARMEST MONTHS
JULY/ AUGUST
38°C

SUNNY DAYS PER YEAR
300

RENEWABLE ENERGY

Almost 40% of heating and cooling on Cyprus uses renewable energy (ninth place in the European Union)

NICOSIA
Biggest city, with 320,000 inhabitants (240,000 in the south and 80,000 in the north)

MOST FAMOUS PEOPLE
Aphrodite
George Michael

OLDEST WINE IN THE WORLD
Commandaria

UNDERSTAND CYPRUS

ANIMAL MAGIC

Cyprus has a rich diversity of fauna and keen naturalists will find plenty to see both during the day and at night. For example, if you see rocks moving around the beach at night, you have not necessarily had one too many glasses of Cypriot wine. It is instead quite likely (especially in June and July) that you are observing turtles burying their eggs on the beach under the cover of darkness. This unique natural spectacle can only be witnessed in a few places in the world – if this tickles your fancy, you can book guided tours of the beaches in Alagadi (p. 117). Pink flamingos by contrast enjoy flaunting themselves in the daytime. They spend the winters on the salt lakes of Lárnaka and Akrotíri, where they enjoy posing for the binoculars and cameras of passing twitchers. Cyprus also has native wild animals. The biggest is the shy mouflon that hides away in the forest in Páfos. The most dangerous is the Levant viper that fortunately does not venture out of the undergrowth.

INSIDER TIP
Put in a night shift with the turtles

FUR COATS IN SUMMER

Cyprus has its cooler spots but is basically very hot in summer. However, don't be surprised to find luxury fur coats for sale in Limassol's smart boutiques. This is because a lot of wealthy Russians live here and a whole economy has sprung up to satisfy their tastes. Of the 40,000 residents from the former Soviet Union who have settled on Cyprus, 75 per cent live in the port. They have their own radio station and newspapers, Russian festivals and a Russian-Orthodox church with gold dome (in Episkopí).

A HARD COFFEE BORDER

Never order a Turkish coffee in the southern part of the island! To Greek-Cypriots mentioning anything Turkish is like a red rag to a bull and in many ways you cannot blame them. In 1974, after a Greek coup to depose the Cypriot president, the Turkish army marched in with bombs and missiles and occupied the northern part of the island; 30,000 soldiers are still stationed there today. Ankara called it a "peace-keeping operation" to protect the minority of Turkish-Cypriots (18%) from the annexation of Cyprus by Greece. The war led to death and expulsions. Ever since, mainly Greek-Cypriots live in the south. The Turkish-Cypriots in the north have established their self-proclaimed state, known as the Turkish Republic of Northern Cyprus, which is only recognised by Turkey. So, if you are in the south and want to enjoy a small mocha, it's better to order a "Cyprus coffee" to avoid annoying the café owner.

THE DIVIDING LINE

On 30 December 1963, Major General Peter Young had had enough. Over

ΦΑΡΜΑΚΕΙΟΝ ΔΙΑΜΑΝΤΗ

Everyday life in Nicosia: coffee beside the Green Line

Christmas, Greek and Turkish Cypriots had clashed in Nicosia and there were fatalities. The commander of British troops sketched a line on the map with a green pen between the residential districts of the conflicting parties intended as a temporary buffer zone to keep the factions apart. No-one (least of all him) would have believed then that 50 years on, the "Green Line" would still exist as a demarcation line in divided Cyprus.

Today, the Green Line runs 217km through the entire country and can only be crossed at seven checkpoints. Since 1964 the UN peacekeeping force (UNFICYP) patrols within the buffer zone, while it is guarded in the north by Turkish soldiers and in the south by the Cypriot national guard.

ANIMAL RESCUE

At last, man can prove that he is dog's best friend – and not just vice versa. Animal-loving holidaymakers can act as "flight companions" and take four-legged strays back to other European countries where new owners are already waiting for them. The initiative is organised by charities such as *CYDRA (cyprusdogsrehomingassociation.com)*. Charities like this rescue hundreds of stray dogs who would otherwise be culled. If you are more of a cat person, there are ways you can help out too. *Monastery Cats (talamonasterycats.com)* offers a home to more than 450 animals and takes any help from volunteers – even if just for a few hours.

INSIDER TIP
Cat hotel

Small but sweet bananas grow in Pafós

HERB GARDEN ON SEA

Bay bushes grow in the park, thyme on the beach and capers by the roadside. Back home, we have these herbs in our spice racks – but in Cyprus, they grow everywhere. Cypriots are fortunate enough to be able to supply all their fruit and vegetable stores with homegrown fruits from the island. The plants are large and small – bananas from Páfos are small but sweet, while watermelons can weigh up to 15kg.

Tall pine and cypress trees grow in the Tróodos mountains, whereas in Akámas the wild orchids are miniature. Incidentally, you will probably be familiar with one early vegetable from the supermarket back home: the Cypriot new potato.

GAMBLING FEVER

The Cypriots are gamblers. There is a betting shop on every corner where punters can bet on horses and football teams. The state and church were strictly against allowing casinos on the south of the island. However, in 2023 a vast hotel and casino complex finally opened in Limassol, with 1,000 gambling machines and 100 tables. Smaller casinos are also planned for Nicosia and Lárnaka. Previously, the Greek Cypriots had squandered their money in casinos in Northern Cyprus. Turkish Cypriots, who, as residents, can't enter casinos in their part of the island, will in future be able to try their luck in the south.

WEDDING FEVER

Not another invitation! In wedding season Cypriots breathe a sigh of relief when the postman walks past their house without stopping. They cannot avoid attending the wedding celebrations of relatives, friends, colleagues and neighbours, which often leave little time for anything else. And it gets expensive. It's not uncommon for there to be several weddings on the same weekend and each comes with financial obligations. After the wedding service, an evening party with family and friends can include up to 2,000 guests. The happy couple, surrounded by parents and siblings, stand in line to receive the congratulations of their guests ... and envelopes stuffed with money. That makes getting married a lucrative investment for young couples! Since all parents wish for the same number of guests at their children's wedding celebrations, they attend all the weddings they are invited to. After all, one good turn deserves another!

DOUBLE MEANINGS

Well, what now? The sign says "Güzelyurt", but on the map the town is called "Morfou". Don't go mad! After the partition of the island, the towns in the north were given Turkish names. But on maps bought in the south, the original names are still listed. On the maps which are available in the north, however, you will find Turkish names for the towns and villages: Páfos is called Baf, for example.

Other towns go by their local names as well as older variations, such as Famagusta near Agía Nápa, which is called Ammóchostos in Greek and Gazimağusa in Turkish. But don't worry, we'll save you from the jungle of names: this MARCO POLO guidebook uses both Turkish and Greek place names for towns in Northern Cyprus.

BLESSINGS (WITH BEER)

In Cyprus, even the saints are greeted with a kiss. Orthodox churchgoers press their lips to the icons as soon as they enter church. If they pass a church, they make a sign of the cross. If they open a business, it must be blessed by the pope. And (almost) every workplace displays the image of a saint. Greek Cypriots are baptised, yet not all are devout. Nevertheless, the church still influences all areas of life, as well as education. As an institution, the church is the island's biggest

TRUE OR FALSE?

THE FRENCH OF THE EAST

Cypriot food is so much more than halloumi and souvlaki. Virtually anything that moves risks ending up on a plate: live snails are sold in the markets; preserved songbirds, although illegal, are still popular; and it is not unusual to see a steamed sheep's head on a restaurant table. There are more easily digestible local delicacies too, such as the custom of eating preserved capers whole with their stalks and even thorns.

THE STREETS BELONG TO ME

It may seem as though the rules of the road don't apply in Cyprus: drivers in the biggest cars assume they have right of way; people park wherever and however they like, while others stop in the middle of the road to chat to friends. Keep your wits about you on Cypriot roads both as a driver and, as a pedestrian.

TRADITION IS OUT

Cypriot women skipping around in colourful traditional dresses, while their husbands strum away on a *bouzoúki*? If this is your idea of life on the island, dream on. Don't be surprised to find a surplus of modern, minimalist cafés, yet not a single village taverna open for business.

landowner and owns shares in companies, including the KEO brewery.

Turkish Cypriots, on the other hand, have a rather indifferent approach to religion. Although they are Muslims, most don't participate in Friday prayers or fast during Ramadan. But mosques are springing up everywhere, largely thanks to the religious practice of Turkish immigrants.

A FRESH PINCH

Cyprus salt has been a lucrative export for centuries. Until it closed in 1986, workers at the salt works in Lárnaka raked this "white gold" into pyramids on the salt lake before selling it across the island ... and further afield. The hot summer sunshine helps the water to evaporate and a white salt crust remains. This crunches underfoot when you walk over it. Only one of the old salt companies is still trading and today produces a refined product made of sea salt: pyramid salt for connoisseurs.

UNIVERSITY CHALLENGE

Greek Cypriots are drawn to studying in Greece, while Turkish Cypriots often head to Turkey – and both are equally keen on attending university in the UK or USA. There are also dozens of colleges and universities in Cyprus.

Two minarets were added, and Nicosia's St Sophia Cathedral became the Selimiye Mosque

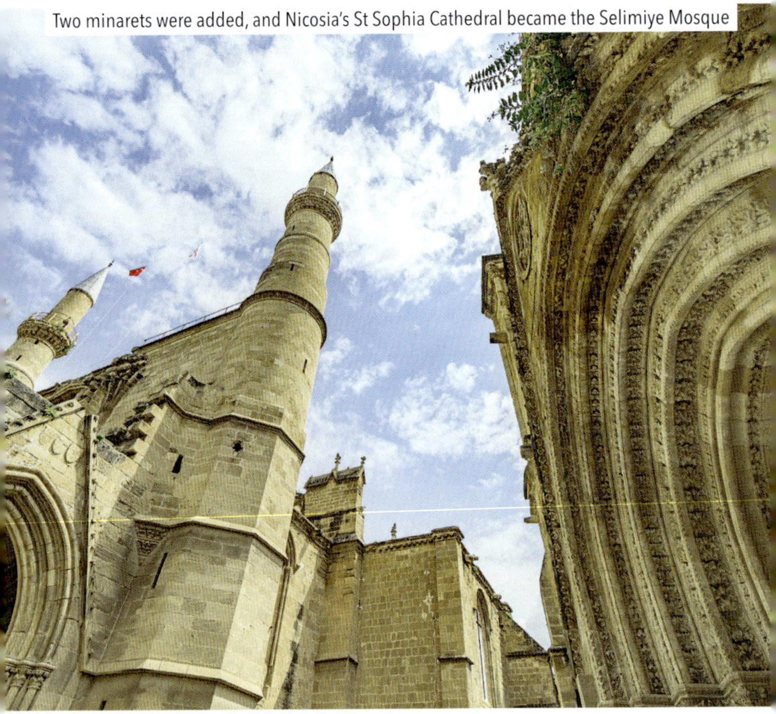

However, in the south's numerous institutions, almost 60% of the students are international, while in the North an entire business sector has grown up catering to foreign students. In fact, tuition fees from international students at the 18 universities in Northern Cyprus make up 35% of GDP.

ALL HEROES AND SAINTS

Don't burst out laughing if an old grandma is called "Aphrodite" or a lanky guy is called "Achilles". The names of classical gods and heroes are still popular on Cyprus. Greek Cypriots' most popular names for their children are Maria and Andreas. Almost all children receive at least one name borrowed from the Bible or later Christian tradition. Their saint's name day is celebrated annually and is more important than their actual birthday. All those who have not been named after a Christian saint and therefore have no "name day" can still celebrate – on All Saints' Day.

CAMPAIGN AGAINST BIRD HUNTING

A tradition has become a major business. Blackcaps captured with lime twigs used to be a meagre foodstuff for smallholder farmers. But with time, poachers began targeting the songbirds and selling the *ambelopouli* to restaurants that serve them as a delicacy. Trapping birds is now illegal, so the dealers achieve even higher prices. A dozen songbirds on a plate usually costs about 80 euros. Every year, more than 2 million songbirds perish on Cyprus. Animal rights groups from other European countries have become involved in the fight to curb illegal bird poaching. Holidaymakers can do their part to put an end to the bird mafia by giving a wide berth to any restaurant whose menu features the *ambelopouli* as a speciality.

LAYERS OF ARCHITECTURE

Demolition and rebuilding is costly. That was also the view of many of the foreign rulers over the centuries who took control on Cyprus. They simply used their predecessors' grand buildings and added their own touch.

From the year 330, the Byzantines established their churches on the remains of ancient temples (such as Agía Pareskevi in Geroskípou); from 1192 the Franks built their castles on Byzantine monasteries (for example, St Hilárion near Kerýneia); and from 1571 the Ottomans built their minarets on cathedrals.

St Sophia's Cathedral in Nicosia became the Selimiye Mosque and the Cathedral of St Nicholos in Famagusta became Lala Mustafa Pasha Mosque – these two churches were used for coronations and, perhaps as a result, their transformation was of particular importance to the Ottomans. The administrative buildings from the British colonial era (from 1878) continued to be used by the independent Republic of Cyprus (from 1960). Government House in Nicosia, for example, was used as the presidential palace, while the former press office became a parliament building, and in Lárnaka the police station … remained a police station.

EATING SHOPPING SPORT

Grilled halloúmi as a salad topping: only real if it squeaks when you eat it

EATING & DRINKING

MULTICULTURAL HERITAGE

Cypriot cuisine is the product of its history: centuries of incomers have added their own dishes to the local traditional food, resulting in a cuisine marked by a blend of hearty, homely cooking using spices from all over the world. Try and spot the influences on everything you eat, be they Turkish or Middle Eastern, Italian or Asian, or even … British.

REGIONAL CUISINE

In an era where our food's sustainability matters, Cyprus has good and bad news to share. On the positive side, almost everything you eat will have been locally sourced. The bad news is that those trying to eat less or no meat will have problems here. Meat often comes in the form of lamb or goat (*kléftiko*) and is still sometimes cooked in a traditional clay oven, although spit roasts above a charcoal grill have become much more popular. Pulses are popular both in cold and warm dishes; in salads you can find all kinds of green leaves – from fresh coriander to wild herbs. A lot of vegetables are also eaten raw or pickled (such as caper twigs).

LADEN TABLES

Do you want to try everything right away? That's no problem! You should order a mezé (pronounced "may-zay"). This usually consists of 12 or 20 different dishes – from olives or sausage pickled in wine to snails – served on small plates; there's something for everyone. If you want a taste of the sea, there is often the option of a fish *mezé*. Cypriot menus often have a traditional warming winter soup: trahanás; a sun-dried mixture of shredded wheat and yoghurt is used as a kind of stock cube. The hard pieces are softened in water and boiled to a thick soup, then

Must tries: Cypriot meze dishes (left) and local cheese (right)

enriched with halloumi. *Trahanás* cubes make an ideal edible souvenir to take home with you.

QUENCHING YOUR THIRST

In the south, good food is always accompanied by a good local wine. For a refreshing drink try the local beer. In addition to the main brands like Keó and Carlsberg, or Efes in the north, it's worth trying some of the creative craft beers made in the island's microbreweries.

Before a meal, people commonly drink a local sherry or brandy. And if you are after a digestif afterwards, try the bitter orange liqueur Fílfar, a dessert wine like Commandaría or the traditional Cypriot schnapps Zivania.

In summer, a popular thirst quencher in Northern Cyprus is *ayran*, a mixture of water and yoghurt with some salt and dried peppermint. Freshly squeezed orange juice and home-made lemonade are a must in this land of citrus fruits.

HOTELS, TAVERNAS & FINE DINING

The standard of cooking at Cypriot hotel restaurants is generally high. Traditional dishes and local ingredients have recently been rediscovered (and reinterpreted) by hotel chefs. In some hotels Cypriot breakfast, with bread, halloumi and eggs, is becoming ever more popular. Even in places where the full English is still the breakfast of choice, there are always Cypriot options later in the day. However, many establishments prefer to set up a dinner buffet with different themes that have little to do with Cyprus. Better to visit local tavernas.

A kebab to go or maybe a fine set-course meal? If you choose to dine out, options are plentiful. Every group of immigrants has brought their own culinary secrets to Cyprus. If you want a quiet night in, there are plenty of takeaway and delivery options. For something local and traditional, however, you can venture into a traditional taverna or a more modern temple to Cypriot cooking. In the former you can enjoy authentic home-style cooking, while in the latter you can discover creations by young Cypriot chefs, who combine their skills with traditional, locally sourced ingredients. Most restaurants are open from noon until 3pm and for dinner from 7pm to 11pm.

SUGAR FIEND?

Once you're in, you may never find your way out! The cake shops on Cyprus are temples of temptation with pretty much everything a sweet tooth could possibly desire from Middle Eastern cakes to delicious mousses. Larger bakeries often have a range of takeaway meals, offering local specialities such as *souvla* and grilled salmon alongside more exotic fare like Asian stir-fries. These bakeries are called *sacharoplastío* in Greek and *pastahane* in Turkish. Fruits marinated in sugar syrups can be particularly tempting. Be they cherries, unripened walnuts, bergamot oranges, plums or even melon skin and aubergines, these little treats are unmissable for any sugar addict! The collective term for all these treats served on a small plate with a teaspoon and cake fork is *gliká tou koutoulioú*.

INSIDER TIP
Takeaway feasts

Baklava is super-sweet, sticky and fragrant

COFFEE FOR EVERYONE!

Traditionally, the coffee houses or *kafeníon* (Turkish *kahvehani*) are reserved for men – ideally men who like playing *távli* (backgammon), reading newspapers and debating local and global politics. There is little on offer in terms of drinks except – of course – coffee. You can forget instant Nescafé. Drink like the Cypriots do and order a traditional coffee: you ask for a *café* and explain how you like it: *skétto* (Turkish *sadez*) – without sugar; *métrio* (Turkish *orta*) – with a little sugar; *warígliko* (Turkish *sekerli*) – with a lot of sugar. A frappé – a cold, frothy coffee made with ice cubes and flavoured with milk and sugar – is as ubiquitous as sunglasses in the Cypriot summer.

Today's Specials

Starters

HALLOÚMI
Cypriot cheese made with sheep's and goat's milk, eaten raw or grilled

LOÚNTZA
Cured pork tenderloin served in thin slices

DOLMÁDES
Vine leaves stuffed with rice and/or mincemeat

TAHÍNI
A thick sauce or dip made of sesame, olive oil, garlic, lemon juice

Main Courses

SOUVLÁKI
Small kebabs with bite-sized pieces of pork or chicken

STIFÁDO
A meaty, red wine stew with lots of onions, cinnamon and cumin

IMAM BAYILDI
Braised, stuffed aubergines – the name means, "the imam fainted"

Desserts

BOURÉKIA
Sweet pastries filled with local cream cheese and honey

LOUKOUMÁDES
Fried dough balls bathed in honey

MACHALEPI
A creamy pudding served in rose water

BAKLAVA
Thin sheets of puff pastry doused in lots of sugar syrup and honey

Drinks

CYPRIOT WINE
Look out for Cyprus's native grape types: Mavro, Maratheftiko, Ophthalmó (red); Xynistéri (white)

BRANDY SOUR
An aperitif made from brandy, citrus fruit juice, Angostura bitters, ice and soda. This internationally renowned cocktail was invented on Cyprus in the 1940s

LEMONADE
Home-made from locally sourced lemons

CYPRUS
CYPRUS

SHOPPING

APHRODITE'S BEAUTY PRODUCTS

On the island of Aphrodite, the goddess of beauty, cosmetics are a must. Skin creams made with donkey's milk, which you can purchase at Golden Donkeys Farm in Skarínou, are particularly popular. Our top tip is 'Cleopatra's Serum', which helps rejuvenate sun-damaged skin. Olive soaps and creams are bestsellers and also available in souvenir shops. Don't forget to try the products made with rose water. The petals are freshly picked and distilled and then made into face balms, shampoo and creams. You can buy authentic products at the *Rose Factory* in Agrós.

INSIDER TIP
Boost your skin with donkey milk

CERAMIC SOUVENIRS

Everybody is busy taking pictures of food, but what about the plates it is served on? Enter the potter. You can add a touch of vintage to your kitchen with one of the ceramic items made from local clay. Centuries of local craft knowledge go into creating the beautifully designed and decorated pottery. And did you know that, because of evaporation, water stays cold in clay pots, even without ice?

TASTY TREATS

Fill your suitcase with lots of delicious food. Cyprus's Mediterranean cuisine has plenty of treats to offer. For sweet-lovers there's carob syrup, *soujouko* ("snakes" made from almonds and wine syrup) or *loukoumi* (jelly treats). And for the savoury-toothed, there's *halloumi* (cheese that tastes as good cooked as raw) and *pastourma* (sausage preserved in red wine). And then, of course, there's Commandaria, the oldest continually produced wine in the world.

CYPRUS
CYPRUS

Buy a mini-Cyprus to put on your fridge back home

TAILOR-MADE

Why not have a favourite item custom made? Clothes, bags or shoes – all made to your design. Bring a picture or other pattern and choose the material in the shop. Including fitting, production takes up to ten days, so you should order the item at the start of your trip. There are tailors in every town. For shoes you should head for *Lydias Shoes* (Limassol) and *Kelpis Shoes* (Páfos). Fabulous bags are made at *Pana's Bag* (Limassol).

HOMEWARE

You'll find some real gems in small household stores. They sell items that have offered simple solutions to everyday issues faced by Cypriots for hundreds of years: handwoven bread baskets that are hung from the ceiling to keep them away from mice; "shelf cages" that protect charcuterie and cheese from insects; and clay urns to burn sweet-smelling incense. With a bit of creativity, these everyday items can be turned into stylish additions to your home. If you're looking to zhuzh up your bathroom at home, Cyprus's long-established craft scene has just the thing for you: loo-roll holders just like your grandma's. Whether you go for the crocheted or knitted version, these will add some welcome kitsch to any bathroom.

JEWELLERY

You can never have enough necklaces and earrings! The island's many jewellery shops offer elegant and classic designs as well as chains sold by the metre. However, you may prefer to visit a boutique run by more modern designers whose creations range from chic to idiosyncratic (located in the popular shopping districts). Or go classical and plump for a replica of ancient jewellery from a museum shop.

SPORT & ACTIVITIES

If you find it hard to sit still, even on holiday, Cyprus is the place for you. The range of activities available is huge and diverse. From swimming to skiing, there is something for everyone and, because the island is small, it is easy to do a lot in one trip. You can spend the morning on the beach before heading into the mountains in the afternoon.

BEACH VOLLEYBALL

With so many sandy beaches, beach volleyball is an obvious choice of sport. Many hotels have set up their own courts. You can also watch the pros play in the international competitions held on the palm-lined promenade in Lárnaka *(FB: Larnaka Beach Volley)*.

BIKING

Well-marked cycling paths are found throughout the south. If you are interested in hiring bikes or booking tours, go to *cyprusactive.com*. Bike-hire experts like *ZypernBike (zypernbike.com)* or *Bikecyprus (bikecyprus.ch)* are also good places to get started with rental equipment or guided tours. For independent cycling you can put together your own routes with the help of the brochure "Cyprus Cycling Routes", available in tourist information offices or online at *visitcyprus.com*.

Mountain-bike races are held several times a year and are open to amateurs as well as the pros. *The Cyprus Cycling Federation (cypruscycling.org)* organises non-profit mountain-bike tours, which are mainly enjoyed by Cypriots. In Northern Cyprus, mountain-bike enthusiasts tend to head to the Kerýneia mountains or the Karpass peninsula.

CLIMBING

Cyprus is home to lots of fabulous wild and remote climbing spots, including

Cyprus's south coast has the ideal conditions for windsurfing

bolted climbs in the grounds of a monastery, an abseiling tower belonging to the national guard, sandstone rocks by the sea, cliffs with spectacular views and bouldering routes in a national park. If you're new to climbing, you're best off booking a slot with an instructor in the *Adventure Mountain Park (adventuremountain park.com)* in Kyperoúnta. For more information on climbing in the south, go to *cyprusrocks.eu*, and for the north, head to *northcyprusclimbing.com*.

INSIDER TIP
Supervised climbing

DIVING

The warm water temperatures mean the diving season on Cyprus lasts from March into November, making it one of the longest in the Mediterranean. Underwater caves, shipwrecks and the remains of ancient amphorae make for great adventures. Diving schools and operators can be found in all the beach resorts on Cyprus. Particularly appealing are the dives near Lárnaka, where the wreck of the 197 m-long freighter *Zenobia* lies on the seabed, or the ruins of the submerged ancient city of Sálamis.

Decompression chambers are available within a 30-minute drive from all dive sites *(diving.org.cy)*. Many diving centres, including *Dive In* in Limassol *(dive-in.com.cy)* and *Taba Diving Centre (tabadiving.com)* offer ☂ trial lessons for beginners. More information can be found online at *visitcyprus.com* or *cyprusdivingcentre.com*.

FISHING

Cyprus is a paradise for those who love to fish. Organised fishing trips on boats are offered from Lárnaka and Páfos. Deep-sea fishing fans can book excursions on specially equipped boats in almost all the larger coastal towns. The

16 reservoir lakes on Cyprus are perfect for freshwater fishing. Check with the local tourist office for information about fishing licences (17–36 euros).

GOLF

Cyprus is a year-round golf destination. For the best experience head to one of its 18-hole courses, all of which are breathtaking. Many are located in the southwest, near Páfos: *Mínthis Hills Golf Club (minthisresort.com/resort/golfclub), Secret Valley Golf Club (secretvalleygolfclub.com), Aphrodite Hills Golf Course (aphroditehills.com)* and *Eléa Estate (eleaestate.com)*. In Northern Cyprus, the *Korineum* at the *Cyprus Golf & Beach Resort (korineum golf.com)* at Esentepe also has an 18-hole course, while the *CMC Golf Club (FB: Cyprus Mediterranean Coast Golf Club)* in Yeşilyurt is the oldest on the island.

HIKING

Most of the numerous well-marked hiking and nature trails can be found in the Tróodos mountains and on the Akámas peninsula. They are often laid out as circular walks. Guided tours in the Tróodos mountains are often run by hotels and guesthouses.

The *European long-distance path E4* runs for over 539km through the south of Cyprus. Individual legs of the path as well as other hiking trails are outlined online at *visitcyprus.com* and written guides are available from tourist offices. There are also marked hiking trails in Northern Cyprus. Good guided walks are on offer from *North Cyprus Walks (northcypruswalk.com)*.

KITESURFING

Cyprus is considered to be something of a hidden secret among kitesurfers. There are countless water-sports centres that offer kitesurfing all year round. The best beaches are Avdimou, Lady's Mile, Kitemed (Pervolia) and Paramali in the south, and Akdeniz in the north.

MARATHON/TRIATHLON

Tough (and very fit) runners and triathletes are often drawn to Cyprus. In March, there is a range of long- (above 10km) and short-distance events on offer for people who have trained through the winter. The major draw on the island for runners from all over the world is the *Limassol International Marathon (limassol marathon.com)*, whose route takes competitors along the coast. In June, the night run, *Run under the Moon*, in Nicosia is also very popular *(running underthemoon.com)*. Triathletes have also discovered Cyprus – outdoor training is possible all year round, and the *Agía Nápa Race (ayianapatriathlon.com)* in March is the first race of the year in Europe.

PARAGLIDING

A unique opportunity for tandem paragliding on the island is offered by *Highline Air Tours (office on the Kerýneia/Girne harbour | highline paragliding.com | allow approx. 2 hrs)*. A minibus will take you from your hotel to the starting point at an altitude of 750m near St Hilárion Castle. During the flight, there are spectacular views down to the town below before you come in to land right by the sea.

The most popular spot for paragliding in the south is the jagged coast around *Koúrion (tandem flights from cyprusflyadventures.com)*. If you are able to fly alone, there is lots of information at *paraglidingmap.com/countries/cyprus*.

RIDING

There are only a handful of professionally run stables offering hacks as well as lessons. Most of them are based in the area around *Páfos (aphrodite hills.com/riding-club, mariashorses.com)*. They offer everything from one-hour hacks to multiple-day tours into the countryside. For more information or stables in other regions, visit the local tourist offices.

SKIING

Between Christmas and the end of February, the slopes of Mount Ólympos, at altitudes of over 1,700m, often have enough snow for skiing. You can hire skis and boots at the hut run by the *Cyprus Ski Club*. For more information and to check the local webcams, head to *cyprusski.com*.

WINDSURFING

Opportunities for windsurfing and many other water sports are available at nearly all major beach hotels. Cyprus's south coast boasts a number of beaches that are ideal for windsurfing. The best spots are located between Páfos in the west and Agía Nápa in the east. The bays of Pissoúri and Koúrion, as well as the beach called Lady's Mile, come well recommended. Most of the surfing centres in Northern Cyprus sit along the coast to the west of Kerýneia and near Sálamis.

YOGA

Although the yoga trend is still low-key on Cyprus, there is still a lot of demand for the courses and retreats that are on offer. In the mountain village of Tochni, the resort *Cyprus Villages (cyprusvillages.com.cy)* organises ayaga teaching courses in addition to its normal classes. The *AcroYoga Community (FB: AcroYoga Cyprus)* promises to combine relaxation with acrobatic power in various locations on the island..

There are stunning dive sites all around the Cypriot coast

REGIONAL OVERVIEW

Girne
Keryneia
(Kyrenia)
Experience the every-day craziness of a divided capital
Güzelyurt
Morfou
LEFKOŞA
LEFKOSÍA
(NICOSIA)
Follow in the footsteps of the goddess of love
NICOSIA p. 64
Tróodos
PÁFOS p. 80
TRÓODOS p. 96
Páfos
LIMASSOL p. 54
Lemesos
(Limassol)
Hang out with the rich and beautiful at the marina
20 km
12.43 mi

Mesógeios Thálassa
(Mediterranean Sea)
Dipkarpaz
Rizokarpaso
Escape the crowds in unspoilt natural landscapes
NORTHERN CYPRUS p. 108
Vadili
Vatili
Party until dawn in one of Europe's nightlife capitals
Agía Nápa
Lárnaka
AGÍA NÁPA & LÁRNAKA p. 38
Sample Cypriot wine in a shady mountain village

AGÍA NÁPA & LÁRNAKA

FOR PARTY ANIMALS & SUN WORSHIPPERS

The southeastern corner of Cyprus is a temple dedicated to one deity: holidays. Nature gifted it with pristine, white beaches and turquoise sea and the locals do their utmost to make sure they provide the rest, from comfy beds to all-night beach parties.

The region is renowned for its breathtaking coastal scenery and small holiday resorts. In the summer, Agía Nápa becomes a party capital. If this spring break mentality is too lively for you, you can always retreat to Paralímni-Protarás for a more relaxed beach holiday.

Nature has sculpted the shoreline at Cape Gréko

The bays and beaches around Cape Gréko and Lárnaka are popular all year round with the diving and kitesurfing communities. When the heat dies down in spring and autumn, tourists can explore the largely flat area on bikes.

In Lárnaka, you'll find the holiday holy trinity: resort, beach and sea. You can swim on one side of the palm-fringed promenade or chill in a café on the other side. Behind the old town's fortress, the promenade stretches out to the fishing port and clubs on Mackenzie Strip.

AGÍA NÁPA & LÁRNAKA

Düzova
Ulukışla
Λευκωσία
Lefkoşa
Nicosia
Gaziköy
Paşaköy
Pasakoy
Kırklar
Vadili
Vatili
Στρόβολος
Strovolos
Γέρι
Geri
CYPRUS
ΚΥΠΡΟΣ - KIBRIS
Akdoğan
A1
Tseri
Athienou/Kiracıköy
Athienou
Ποταμιά
Potamia
Marki
Dali
Pýla 9
Lympia
Ayia Varvara
Oroklini
Alampra
A2
Αραδίππου
Aradhippou
Oróklini Lake 8
Mosfiloti
Livadia
Λυθροδόντας
Lythrodontas
40km, 45 mins
Kalo Chorio
Lárnaka
p. 47
7 Salt lake
A1
Δρομολαξιά
Dromolaxia
Lefkara
Lefkara
A5
13 Páno Léfkara
Anglisides
Κίτι
Kiti
Golden Donkeys Farm
10 Cape Kíti
14
Kofinou
Skarinou
Pervolia
Mazotos
11 Camel Park
15 Choirokoitía (Khirokitia)
Archaeological site
16 Tochní
A1
Μαρώνι
Maroni
Μαρί
Mari
12 Zýgi
6 km
3.73 mi

Alaniçi
gizli
Mormenekşe
Yeniboğaziçi
Dörtyol
Mutluyaka
Tuzla
Kolpos Ammochostou
önü
onu
Gazimağusa
Famagusta
Köprülü
Güvercinlik
Δερύνεια
Deryneia
İncirli
15km, 20 mins
3 Derínia (Derýneia)
50km, 40 mins
Avgorou
Frenaros
2 Paralímni-Protarás
Παραλίμνι
Paralimni
5 Frénaros
Flour Museum
ylotympou
Cyherbia
Herb Park 6
Liopetri
Fig Tree Bay
Protaras
Ορμήδεια
Ormideia
Ξυλοφάγου
Xylofagou
Makronissos
Beach
Níssi
Beach
Agía Nápa
p. 42
Kónnos Bay
Pótamos
tou Liopetríou 4
Kolpos Lárnakas
Cape Gréko (Akrotírio Gkréko) 1
Mesógeios Thálassa
(Mediterranean Sea)

MARCO POLO HIGHLIGHTS

★ **CAPE GRÉKO**
The best sunsets on the island ➤ p. 44

★ **SALT LAKE**
A dazzling plain of white crystals which attracts colourful visitors in winter ➤ p. 51

★ **PÁNO LÉFKARA**
This picture-postcard village is where the famous *lefkarítika* lace is made ➤ p. 53

★ **GOLDEN DONKEYS FARM**
Organic donkey milk cosmetics from a farm shop ➤ p. 53

★ **CHOIROKOITÍA ARCHAEOLOGICAL SITE**
See how people on Cyprus lived 8,000 years ago ➤ p. 53

RESTAURANT FRESH
BEERS ICE CREAM
COFFEES

Agía Nápa's little harbour is full of tavernas serving freshly caught fish

AGÍA NÁPA

(□ 07) **Agía Nápa is seen as the island's coolest corner. The party crowd turns the nights into days (which in these temperatures is just as well!).**

Every year in high season, the small coastal town with a population of 3,000 is turned into a summer metropolis. From May to October, 350,000 guests find their way here. The coast has, however, managed to remain free from the worst excesses of the kind of architecture that usually goes with budget tourism. Even better, there are no private beaches here, so you can spend your days at the beach without having to worry about bringing your wallet. In the evening, the fishing port and monastery are a great spot for a sundown stroll on your way to one of the towns many restaurants. As long as it's light, Agía Nápa feels like a family-friendly resort. Later on, however, it's party time on the streets and squares. From October, the place enters a kind of hibernation with mainly hikers, birdwatchers and pensioners enjoying the relaxing peace and quiet.

SIGHTSEEING

AGÍA NÁPA MONASTERY

This overcrowded spot was once a secret hideaway. When religion was still banned, a small Christian community used to meet in the rock cave

– today there is an underground church on the site. The 600-year-old sycamore tree in front of the monastery – one of Cyprus's oldest trees – makes a great subject for a photo, especially when the old men from the village are seated in front of it. *Free admission during the day | in the centre, on the main street leading to the fishing port*

MUSEUM THÁLASSA

Did the ancient Greeks really dare to go out on the high seas in that tiny papyrus boat? The very thought of it may bring on a bout of seasickness. On the other hand, the maritime museum's star attraction, an ancient trading ship, is a giant. This is a seaworthy replica of the original vessel from Kerýneia that sunk 2,300 years ago. *Mon & Sat 9am–2pm, Tue–Fri 9am–5pm | admission 4 euros | Krío Neró 14 | 1 hr*

SCULPTURE PARK

At last, art that you can touch! At the open-air sculpture park, you can poke an owl in the eye and clamber up onto the mermaid's fin. Your challenge, should you choose to accept it, is to take the most imaginative photo possible here. The hillside on which the park sits is on the eastern edge of the town and has no shade whatsoever. As a result, it's better to visit in the early morning or in the evening. *Open 24/7 | free admission | 30 mins*

INSIDER TIP Don't go at midday!

EATING & DRINKING

ESPERIA

Listen to the splashing waves over dinner (downstairs) or look up to Cape Gréko (upper terrace). Both are as irresistible as the freshly caught fish! *Daily 11am–11pm | Leofóros Archiepiskópou Makáriou III 46| €€–€€€*

NÁPA

One of the first tavernas established in the town. Instead of writing in a guestbook, generations of customers have left witty comments on the walls. The food is as charmingly rustic and traditional as the interior. *Daily 5.30–11pm | Odós Dimokratías 15 | above the monastery | tavernanapa1976.com | €€*

SPORT & ACTIVITIES

On the beaches in this region, there is no shortage of diving schools or huts offering wakeboarding, water-skiing … and much more besides.

WATERWORLD

This water park at one end of Agía Nápa's beach allows adults a brief return to their childhood. We defy even the most strait-laced grown-up not to come out in whoops and giggles while hurtling down its 150m-long slides. If you book go-kart tickets at the same time, you save 3 euros *(EMW Go Karts, 20 euros/10 mins). May–Oct daily 10am–5.30pm | adults 45 euros, children (3–12) 27 euros | Leofóros Agías Théklas | waterworldwaterpark.com |* *07*

BEACHES

You won't have any trouble finding beaches in Agía Nápa, we promise. The nicest are *Níssi Beach*, *Kónnos Bay*, *Fig Tree Bay*, *Green Bay*, *Makronissos Beach* and *Agía Thékla*. The most popular way to get to the beaches is on quad bikes or scooters but there are also buses. The city beaches in Agía Napa offer free Wifi.

NIGHTLIFE

BED ROCK INN

Wilmaaaaa! Flintstone flair on the outside, funky on the inside, with "Yabba Napa Doo" parties and wet T-shirt contests that may not be suitable for all the family. Headphones are available for a silent disco, and the shop sells leopard-skin clothing. *Daily from 8pm | Ippokratous 2, corner of Odós Loúka Loúka | bedrockinn.com*

CARWASH DISCO

Do you want to really let your hair down? Cheesy hits from the 1970s and 80s that get stuck in your head but get people of all ages onto the dancefloor. *Daily 2pm–6am | Odós Ayiás Mávris 39 | FB: Carwash Disco.*

PARK PALIATSO

What is more fun than joining the crowds at the fair? Flashing lights, music, cocktails and scream-inducing rides. There are also traditional carousels for kids. *Daily 6pm–midnight | adults 25 euros (22 rides), children 10 euros (9 rides) | Leofóros Níssi | parkopaliatsocy.com*

AROUND AGÍA NÁPA

If you are staying in or around Agía Nápa and Paralímni-Protarás, it is a good idea to buy a weekly bus ticket. For 20 euros, you will be able to get to all the beaches and villages in the area as well as to the waterpark and Cape Gréko – it will even take you as far as Lárnaka. Find timetables in tourist information offices and online at *osea.com.cy* (for Agía Nápa). For Lárnaka buses, go to *inonasbuses.com.*

1 CAPE GRÉKO (AKROTÍRIO GKRÉKO) ★

6km / 15 mins from Agía Nápa by car (on arrival there is a steep walk up to the viewing platform)

First, watch the sunset from the cliffs. Then, watch couples posing for their wedding pics against the red backdrop! The top of the peninsula is off limits due to the presence of military installations, but there are numerous options for detours to rocky coves, grottos and sandy beaches (see p. 127). *07*

2 PARALÍMNI-PROTARÁS

6km / 10 mins from Agía Nápa by car

Protarás is pretty much the dictionary definition of summer holidays. Apart from beaches, hotels, restaurants and entertainment, nothing here prevents you from lazing around. The coastal resorts of Protarás and *Pernéra* stretch beyond the village of Paralímni, 5km north of Agía Nápa. The village square (with its three churches) provides an opportunity for tourists who want to meet the locals – either in the bars and restaurants or in the traditional village festivals. The best spot for an amazing panoramic shot is in front of the chapel that sits on a rock known as *Profítis Ilías* on the western edge of Protarás. Four "wishing trees" are right next to the chapel. In the past, devout visitors knotted handkerchiefs to these trees to support their prayers. Today, tourists add trainers and even underwear.

You are unlikely to find so many perfect beaches so close together anywhere else in the Mediterranean. The sea is crystal clear and incredibly blue. You'll probably want to spend the whole day in it either swimming, snorkelling, riding speed boats or partaking in a host of other fun activities. Join a boat tour to see the coast from the water at least once. This always includes a break for a swim, ideally around the *sea caves*. On longer trips you can enjoy the bar and restaurant on board. If you want to bring the little ones with you, *Mermaid Cruises* are designed for kids to come too *(Sat 2pm | 25 euros, children under 12, 15 euros | jetty in Protarás | FB: The Mermaid Cruise)*. They will spend two happy hours in the company of mermaids and pirates while you relax. *07*

3 DERÍNIA (DERÝNEIA)

10km / 15 mins from Agía Nápa by car

A glimpse of a ghost town. From the lookout point of the *Cultural Centre of Occupied Ammóchostos (Mon–Fri 7.30am–4.30pm, Sat 9.30am–4.30pm | free admission)*, you can look directly across to Turkish-occupied Varósha:

The more eye-catching your parasol, the easier it is to find your towel on Níssi Beach

The Lazarus Church in Lárnaka has a magnificent iconostasis with remarkable carvings

7km of beaches, empty buildings and hotels, the resort was abandoned in 1974 and has only been partially reopened since 2022. Derýneia is like a little paradise lost. For a less depressing history lesson, visit the *Derýneia Folkloric Museum (Mon–Sat 9am–1pm, 3–6pm | admission 2 euros | Odós Demetri Liberti 2/3 | deryneia.org.cy | ⏲ 30 mins)* in the centre of town. The old farmer's house has been lovingly restored and furnished and in the garden you'll find a wide range of traditional tools. If you are in the mood for a rustic meal, then, try the historic taverna *O Dikos Mas Mezes (Mon–Sat 6–11pm | Athinón Street 2 | €€)* in the centre of the village, which also serves vegan food.

If you cross into Northern Cyprus at Derýneia, you will reach Famagusta in just 6km. To get to Derýneia, you can take buses from Agía Nápa (no. 502 via Paralímni) and from Protarás (no. 708 also via Paralimni). There are taxi ranks on both sides of the green line by the checkpoint. You should encounter no problems crossing the border in a car or on a bike. *N6*

4 PÓTAMOS TOU LIOPETRÍOU

10km / 15 mins from Agía Nápa by car

Idyllic! This attractive river port is still pretty unspoilt. Hundreds of small fishing boats are moored here and their daily catch is served fresh in the local tavernas. If you are not afraid of early starts (the boats normally set off at 4am) see if you can

INSIDER TIP
A day as a fisherman's friend

persuade one of the local fishermen to take you out on a trip for a small fee. *N7*

5 FRÉNAROS FLOUR MUSEUM

18km / 25 mins from Agía Nápa by car

Form an orderly queue! Give milling a go and see how strenuous this once-constant feature of daily life was. The museum is part of a working factory in Frénaros, to the northwest of Agía Nápa. Make the most of this hands-on experience! *Mon–Fri 9am–1pm and 3–6.30pm, Sat/Sun 9am–2.30pm | admission 2 euros | Fotis Pittas 80 | cyprusmillers.com*

INSIDER TIP For the love of melons

If you visit the village in the middle of June, you may well find yourself in the midst of the annual Melon Festival. The locals here love enlightening people about the process of growing and selling melons, so you can learn a lot about this sweetest of fruits. *N7*

6 CYHERBIA HERB PARK

20km / 30 mins from Agía Nápa by car

When the warm summer wind blows across the extremely herby herbaceous borders here, your nose will know about it! From scents to creams and teas, you can buy a range of products made from the plants grown here to take home with you. Meanwhile the kids will have plenty of time to get lost in the maze. *Daily 10am–7pm | entry 5 euros, children (5–12) 3 euros | near Avgórou on the E 311 | cyherbia.com | 1.5 hrs | M–N7*

LÁRNAKA

(L8) **The port town of Lárnaka has something for everyone. Wanna relax on the beach? Why not? Or maybe you'd prefer to showcase your summer wardrobe on the promenade? Feel free! What about some shopping? Or joining a party? It's all possible here.**

Just under an hour from Agía Nápa by bus, Lárnaka has gathered practically all the holiday highlights in one place and you can get everywhere on foot. As this town (pop. 85,000) is one of the oldest in the world, it's worth having a historical snoop around. Start at the bust of Zenon from Kition *(Europe Square on the Palm Promenade)*, the pearl of whose wisdom was that we should live a relaxed life. It may sound like a stoner fantasy, but it is actually the cornerstone of the philosophical teachings of stoicism.

SIGHTSEEING

Love Buses (departure Finikoudes promenade: 11.15am, 5.15pm, in winter 3.15pm | 20 euros | lovebuses cyprus.net | 2.5 hrs) take you to the main sights. In the evening there are tours with music.

LAZARUS CHURCH

It all began with a miracle: Lazarus lay dead in a rocky sarcophagus, then Jesus came and woke him. And ever since, his name has been inextricably linked to reincarnation and miraculous healing. Whether you believe the story

LÁRNAKA
Theo Michael
Art Café 1900
Ancient Kition
Halcoessa Copper Art
Lazarus Church
Old Market St
Finikoúdes Promenade
Fort
Turkish Quarter
Ammos Beach Bar
Nusa Beach Bar
Zephyros Beach Tavern
Kolpos Lárnakas
Stasinou Street
Lordou Vyronos
Galilaiou
Ermou
Agias Elenis
Paraskeva Ioannou
Stylianou Apostolidi Street
Kostaki Pandelidi Street
A. Sourouki
Kostantinou Kalogera Street
Zinonos Kitieos Street
Athinon Avenue
Aisopou Street
Stadiou Street
Diogenous Street
Adonidos Street
Agiou Lazarou Street
Aphroditis St.
Kosma Lysioti St.
P. Valsamaki
Faneromenis Avenue
Touran
Rimni
El Alamein Street
Fleming Street
Pasteur Street
Apolaniou Kitieos Street
Katoli & Georgiou St.
Solon
Mehmet Ali
Piyiale Pasa
Okullar
Selim
Istamboul
200 m
219 yd

or not, Lazarus was a real person and – in his second life – he was the first bishop of Kition (Lárnaka). His skull is still kept in this church and forms part of a shrine to him. Thanks to the bell tower, St Lazarus has become a city landmark and forms the backdrop of the café, taverna and hotel district around the square. *Mon–Sat 8am–6.30pm (winter 8am–12.30pm, 2.30–5pm), Sun 6.30am–12.30pm, 3.30–6.30pm; (winter until 5.30pm) | free admission to church and museum | Ágios Lázaros Street | 30 mins*

FORT

Pole position for photos! From the ramparts of the port's fort (1625) you can enjoy the views up and down the beach. There are often events inside its cannon-lined main court. The old gallows chamber by the main entrance still has a rope swinging in it ... *April–Sept Mon–Fri 8am–7.30pm, Sat/Sun 9.30am–7.30pm; (winter until 5pm) | admission 2.50 euros | waterfront promenade | 30 mins*

FINIKOÚDES PROMENADE

This is where the flaneurs hang out – on the edge of the city with views out to sea. The opposite side of the road is filled with cafés, bars and restaurants. In the evenings, music fills the air, and – for two euros – you can have a peak at the stars from a 🐷 telescope. It doesn't get much more romantic.

TURKISH QUARTER

There can be advantages to a neighbourhood falling on hard times. In the side streets west of the fort, time seems to have stood still. The slanted old houses are a charming sight and, in recent years, they have become a hive of small workshops and studios. The ceramic workshops are of particular note. Don't miss *Emira Pottery (Mon–Fri 8am–9pm, Sat 9am–3pm | Odós Mehmet Ali 13 | emirapottery.com.cy)*. Alongside more artistic pieces, they make beautiful rustic crockery from egg cups to plates and water jugs.

INSIDER TIP **Perfect pots**

ANCIENT KITION

Hippies swear by these stones. The remains of a temple of the goddess Astarte (ninth century BCE) were uncovered here and its said that her presence can still be felt. *April–Sept Mon–Fri 9.30am–5pm (winter 8.30am–4pm) | admission 2.50 euros | Archbishop Kyprianos Av. | 30 mins*

Finikoúdes' perfect promenade has restaurants on one side and the sea on the other

EATING & DRINKING

ART CAFÉ 1900

Nobody visits the 1900 for its food. The place is an institution thanks to its artistic decor, interesting guests and fabulous music. But if you miss out on ordering something from the menu (e.g. chicken in beery gravy) you only have yourselves to blame. The ground-floor bar is famous for the incredible variety of drinks on offer. *Wed–Mon 6pm–2am | 6 Stasinoú Street | FB: Artcafe1900 | €*

NUSA BEACH BAR

Kick back with your feet in the warm sand and a cold drink in your hand. Need we say more? *Mon–Thu 7am–11pm, Fri–Sun until midnight | just behind the fishing port | €*

ZEPHYROS BEACH TAVERN

The freshest fish in all of Lárnaka is served here – the fish meze is superb. The restaurant is right next to the small harbour, and is supplied directly with the catch of the day. Through the panoramic windows you can enjoy the sea view. *Daily 11.30am–10.30pm | Odós Tasoú Mitsopouloú 1 | tel. 24 65 71 98 | FB: Zephyros Beach Tavern | €€*

SHOPPING

HALCOESSA COPPER ART

Traditional household appliances are stacked next to vintage decorations and antiques, and most of the pieces are actually made of copper. Great for browsing! *Mon/Tue, Thu–Fri 9.30am–7pm, Wed 9.30am–5pm, Sat/Sun 10.30am–6pm | Odós Kleánthi Kalogerá | FB: Halcoessa Copper Art*

THEO MICHAEL ☂

In his studio in the new town you can watch artist Theo Michael at work, take classes with him or have your portrait done in various techniques – pencil drawings, for example, start at 65 euros. Or you can simply admire his work. *Mon–Fri 10am–5pm, Sat 10am–1pm | Odós 5 Agías Elénis | theomichael.co.uk*

BEACHES

If the city beach is too crowded, make a getaway on bus no. 425. It leaves every half-hour from the palm-fringed promenade and makes its way to the long but narrower beaches west and east of the town. Flat and sandy, they are perfect for children.

NIGHTLIFE

AMMOS BEACH BAR

The "in" place to party in Lárnaka, with a range of music from downbeat chill to house. Cocktails and good food. *Daily from 11am | Makenzy Beach | ammos.eu | €€*

OLD MARKET ST

Where the old market used to be, cocktails are now the main feature. There are tables outside in the alley-way, so you get to soak up the atmosphere of a summer night in the old town. *Mon–Thu 6pm–1am, Fri–Sun 6pm–2am | Odós Kleánthi Kalogerá | €€*

Be dazzled by the white of the salt lake or the pink of the flamingos

AROUND LÁRNAKA

7 SALT LAKE ★

2km / 10 mins from Lárnaka by car

Don't forget your sunnies! The salt crust of the lake can be as blinding as snow in the summer sun. If you step on it, it crunches and cracks underfoot like ice. But don't worry, it is salt and won't break! In winter, the lake fills with water ... and pink flamingos.

The best photos get the view across the lake to the *Hala Sultan Tekke Mosque (daily 8.30am–5pm, closed Fri 1–3pm; free admission | 30 mins)* on the other side, with the palm trees behind it serving as a backdrop. The mosque is an important Muslim pilgrimage site. In the year 647, the aunt of the Prophet Muhammad fell from a donkey and died here. Her grave can be visited at the far corner of the mosque. *L8*

8 OROKLINI LAKE

7km / 10 mins by car from Lárnaka

Are you a keen birdwatcher? Next to the motorway between Lárnaka and Agía Nápa is a solitary wooden hut by the lake. From this hide, you can watch the birds as they glide over the water. Keep your camera at the ready! *Coastal rode B3, Exit: Oróklini | 30 mins*

9 PÝLA

20km / 35 mins from Lárnaka by car

See, it can work! While the politicians have been talking for more than 40 years about how to reunite the island, in Pýla it was never divided: Greek and Turkish Cypriots still live next door to each other. The village is situated in the buffer zone administered by the UN, that is to say the no-man's-land between Northern and Southern Cyprus, 9km northeast of Lárnaka. On the village square, sometimes you only notice whether a café is Greek or Turkish when you order a beer: Keó or

Efes. The mosque and church are both open. UN soldiers patrol the streets – in summer, even in shorts; proof if ever it was needed that there is no tension here. L7

10 CAPE KÍTI

20km / 30 mins from Lárnaka by car

Pervolia Beach has become Cyprus's epicentre for the increasingly trendy sport of kitesurfing. Parachutes float above the sea the whole way down the coast. The pros criss-cross the waves, while the surf schools on Cape Kíti and Pervolia, e. g. *Windbandit (windbandit.com)* make sure that newbies have lots of fun too.

Does that sound too strenuous? Why not spend some time gazing out to sea and contemplating the world? A particularly good spot to do so is *Theta Mediterranean (Tue–Thu 6pm–midnight, Fri–Sun from noon | €)*, next to the small lighthouse. From here, you can walk along the coastal path to some quieter beaches with small cafés and bars. L9

11 CAMEL PARK

30km / 40 mins from Lárnaka by car

A visit to the Camel Park gives you some insight into living Cypriot history. Up until the 1950s, merchants on the island still got from A to B on these dromedaries. The park also houses a pool, a small restaurant and a mini museum. It's a lovely place! *Daily 9am–6.30pm | admission 6 euros, children 4 euros (includes use of the swiming pool); camel ride 7.5 euros) | main road from Kíti to Mazótos | camel-park.com | 3 hrs | K9*

12 ZÝGI

40km / 50 mins from Lárnaka by car

You don't need much to be happy! A picturesque harbour to enjoy a stroll, and plenty of fish restaurants and the

Neolithic man lived in roundhouses at Choirokoitía 8,000 years ago

gentle lapping of the waves. If you can persuade a fisherman to take you out with them very early, you can also enjoy a mini adventure. J9

13 PÁNO LÉFKARA ★

40km / 45 mins from Lárnaka by car

Like stepping into a picture postcard! It's well worth wandering through the quaint backstreets in the tiny mountain village. The older women sit with their embroidery work on their laps in the doorways and create the village's famous lace, known as *lefkarítika*. You can buy the lace in the numerous small shops that generally offer silver handcrafted items as well. The village is a popular tourist attraction and busloads of visitors arrive every day. If one of these waves is coming in, take a seat in one of the small cafés and wait for a while until the crowds disperse. J8

INSIDER TIP **Keep calm and have a cuppa**

14 GOLDEN DONKEYS FARM ★

35km / 45 mins from Lárnaka by car

Visit to stock up on cosmetics made with donkey milk. Most people spend time hanging out with the cute donkeys and zombie-like wax figures that show what village life was like in the past. The food in the café is not bad (very meaty). Kids can have a go riding the donkeys. *Daily 9am–7pm, winter 9am–5pm | admission 6 euros, children 4 euros | on the western edge of Skarínou | goldendonkeys.com | 2 hrs | J9*

15 CHOIROKOITÍA (KHIROKITIA)

30km / 40 mins from Lárnaka by car

In Choirokoitía, Mrs Loulla produces the most fantastic halloumi made from fresh milk from her own goats *(daily 10am–5pm | tel. 99 63 93 88)*. Visitors are allowed to watch her as she goes about her craft. Make sure you try the freshly made, warm soft cheese. The taste could be life-changing.

INSIDER TIP **Melts in your mouth**

As you are passing, there is a lot to learn about prehistoric Cypriots at the nearby ★ *Archaeological Site (April–Sept 8.30am–7.30pm, winter 8.30am–5pm | admission 2.50 euros | next to the motorway | 45 mins)*, which has replicas of round huts that stood here 8,000 years ago. The Neolithic settlement is designed like a small archaeological park. Up to 1,000 inhabitants lived in this early community. In the biggest huts (10m in diameter) there was even a mezzanine floor made of timber. J9

16 TOCHNÍ

38km / 50 mins from Lárnaka by car

It is possible to go cycling, hiking and horse riding in the summer heat if you head for the mountains. Nine good hiking trails detailed in *Hiking Map Tochní* (published by Kartographos) start in the small village. Or you can explore the area on bikes available to hire from the small hotel, *Cyprus Villages (cyprusvillages.com.cy)*, which also has a spa and offers yoga courses. Cycle routes available online at *larnaka region.com/thematic-tours-routes*.

LIMASSOL

BIG CITY VIBES & RURAL CHARM

This is the epitome of a port city! From vast cargo ships to luxury yachts, it has it all. Wealth is at home in Limassol (Greek: Lemesós). For many years the money came from shipping. Then, in more recent decades, the city's 180,000 residents were joined by a rich Russian community, hence the skyscrapers, luxury marina and elegant lakeside promenade.

The old town, located in the historical port, has become a hip-and-happening modern neighbourhood while the run-down

Refurbished old buildings provide the stylish setting for Limassol's evening scene

quarter around the market hall is a magnet for partygoers. Old workshops have received a new lease of life as cafés and bars. With its squares, small backstreets and bridges over the water, it has a touch of Venice.

The city is at its busiest during two annual events: Carnival and the Wine Festival. Fortunately, you can get to the mountains in no time to restore calm and a feeling of balance after your dose of urban adrenalin.

LIMASSOL

Μονιάτης
Moniatis
B8
Μαντριά
Mandria
Ayios Mamas
Τριμίκλινη
Trimiklini
Όμοδος
Omodhos
Άρσος
Arsos
Σαλαμιού
Salamiou
Λιμνάτης
Limnatis
Βουνί
Vouni
Μαλλιά
Mallia
Κιδάσι
Kidasi
35km, 1 hr
45km, 55 mins
Πάχνα
Pachna
Κυβίδες
Kivides
1 Alassa
6 Anógyra (Anóyira)
Souni-Zanakia
15km, 40 mins
Alectora
Ayios Thomas
Αυδήμου
Avdimou
Cyprus Wine Museum
Ερήμη
Erimi
Ypsonas
2
A6
5 Pissoúri
Paramali
Kolóssi 3
Kolossi
Koúrion Beach
Koúrion 4
Επισκοπή
Episkopi
Ασώματος
Asomatos
Kolpos Episkopis
Ακρωτήρι
Akrotiri
7
Mesógeios Thálassa

MARCO POLO HIGHLIGHTS

★ **CYPRUS WINE MUSEUM**
The best kind of wine exhibition. Plenty to learn … and even more to taste ➤ p. 62

★ **KOÚRION**
An ancient spa resort, where you can see how the Romans bathed and chilled out ➤ p. 62

Οδου
Odou
Sikopetra
ΑγίοιΒαβατσινιάς
Ayioi Vavatsinias
Ζωαηγή
Zoopigi
Άγιος Κωνσταντίνος
Ayios Konstantinos
Μελίνη
Melini
Arakapas
Lageia
Akapnou
Καλό Χωριό
Kalo Chorio
CYPRUS
ΚΥΠΡΟΣ - KIBRIS
Κελλάκι
Kellaki
Γεράσα
Gerasa
Prastio
Vasa
30km, 50 mins
Ασγάτα
Asgata
Φασούλα
Fassoula
Ακρούντα
Akrounda
Παρεκκλησιά
Parekklisia
Αρμενοχώρι
Armenochori
Πύργος
Pyrgos
Pentakomo
A1
Γερμασόγεια
Yermasoyia
Άγιος Τύχωνας
Ayios Tychonas
Governor's Beach
B8
Dasoúdi Beach
ano Polemidia
Limassol
p. 58
Kolpos Akrotiriou
Lady's Mile Beach
i Environmental
ion Centre
(Mediterranean Sea)
4 km
2.49 mi

★ **ANÓGYRA (ANÓYIRA)**

A village specialising in the production of Cypriot superfoods. Watch the processes, then taste the results ➤ p. 63

LIMASSOL

(🕮 F–G10) **The Pafilia car park next to Limassol's zoo not only offers free parking but also an easy journey into town with the no. 30 bus, which runs every 15 minutes and terminates at the marina (via the old town).**

SIGHTSEEING

MEDIEVAL CASTLE

Unlike royal weddings today, Richard the Lionheart's marriage to Berengaria in 1191 did not attract media attention. Nonetheless, it was a key event in Cyprus's history because it marked the moment that Richard conquered the island and then gave it to the crusaders. The castle's *museum (Mon–Sat 8am–5pm, Sat 9am–5pm, Sun 10am–1pm | admission 4.50 euros | Odós Richardoú & Berengárias | ⏲ 1 hr)* has an excellent collection of objects that vividly bring to life what life was like for the knights and kings in medieval Europe.

CAROB MILL

Industrial chic. The old *carob mill* (1937) is enjoying a second lease of life as a cultural centre: first, grab a freshly brewed beer at the *Draught (daily noon–11pm)*, then take in a temporary exhibition *(lanitisfoundation.org)*, followed by a visit to the *Carob Museum's* permanent exhibition *(daily 10am–8pm | free admission | ⏲ 15 mins)*. Once you've done all of that, you'll need a nice supper. The *Karatello Tavern*, (Mon–Fri 6pm–1am, Sat/Sun noon–1am) next to the floodlit castle, is almost too well located not to collapse into. *Odós Vasilíssis Berengárias*

6X6 CENTRE FOR PHOTOGRAPHY

Three amenities in one: a gallery, photo studio and museum. Historical cameras – from the era when photographers had to tell their subjects to "watch the birdie!" – are displayed alongside modern exhibitions. Creative input and specialist discussion are top of the agenda here. *Mon, Tue, Thu 9am–5pm, Wed, Fri 9am–1.30pm | free admission | 19 Ipeirou Street | centreforphotographyбx6.com | ⏲ 30 mins*

CYPRUS MOTOR MUSEUM

An impressive and eclectic collection, ranging from a Benz motor car from

> **WHERE TO START?**
>
> **Old town**: If you're arriving in the old town from the hotel district on the no. 30 bus, you'll drive along the coastal road up to the Old Harbour roundabout, which is only 150m away from the castle. Car drivers will find pay-and-display car parks along the waterfront promenade right in front of the Old Harbour or on the other side of the street at the big church (you can turn at the roundabout). From here, you can explore the old town and the area around the marina on foot. Start from the promenade.

LIMASSOL
Enso
6x6 Centre for Photography
Kyriakou Oikonomou
Kapodistria
Othonos Kai Amalias
Zenonos
Street
Solono
Agias Filaxeos
Gladstonos
Vragadinou
Pavlou Mela
16th June 1943
Christodoulo Papadaki
Ptolemaion
Anexartisias
Fat Fish
Megalou Alexandrou street
Thrakis
Markou Botsari
Vasileiou Makedonos
Elenis Palaiologinas
Agiou Andreou
Navarinou Street
Thermopylon
28 Oktovric
Guaba Beach Bar
Georgiou Gennadiou
Salaminos
Athinon
Themidos
Christodoulou Chatzipavlou
Simou Menadrou
Saixpir
Enoseos Street
Ellados
Anexartisias
Dasoúdi Beach
Dareinou
Eirinis
Kitiou Kyprianou
Saripolou
Ifigenias
Eleftherias
Ellinon
Street
Andreou
Agiou
Spyrou Araouzou
The Old Neighbourhood
Stoa Phylactou
Lydias Made to Measure Shoes
Sertar
Agkyras
Serdar
Carob Mill
Medieval castle
Kolpos
Akrotiriou
Kioproulouzante
Agias Theklis
Cyprus Motor Museum
Siafi
Free city tour
Limassol Marina
Limassol Marina
Epsilon Resto Bar
200 m
219 yd

INSIDER TIP
Vintage sightseeing

1886) to an old village bus. You can even rent a vintage car for four hours (price depends on the model). *Mon–Fri 9am–5pm, Sat/Sun 10am–6pm, winter daily 10am–5pm | admission 15 euros | Odós Epimitheos 3056 | cyprusmotormuseum.com.cy* | *2.5 hrs*

FREE CITY TOUR

There is a free walking tour of the city on Mondays at 10am. Advance booking is required. *Meeting point: Tourist information in the old port | tel. 25 36 27 56* | *2.5 hrs*

Pelicans love Limassol's beach bars too!

EATING & DRINKING

ENSO

INSIDER TIP
Vegans' paradise

This vegan food bar serves a whole range of plant-based delicacies. *Mon–Fri 8am–4pm, Sat 8am–3pm | Odós Vasilia Michaelides 4A | enso-vegan.com* | €€

EPSILON RESTO BAR

If you're going to dine at the marina, then do it in style and get a taste of high society. Oysters and lobster are top of the menu. There is also a bar with 30 varieties of rum – need we say more? *Daily noon–midnight | Marina | tel. 25 05 13 93 | pns.com.cy* | €€€

FAT FISH

Local spot with a cosy taverna feel and the menu of a gourmet fish restaurant. By the sea, fresh fish, excellent wines. *Daily 12.30–3.30pm, 7–11pm | Promachon Eleftheria 8/1 | tel. 25 82 81 81* | €€

THE OLD NEIGHBOURHOOD

Let's hope this place never changes! The fish taverna is so old that it is already retro. Only the catch of the day is served. The locals proudly invite their guests here. *Mon–Sat from 7pm | Odós Ángyras 14* | €

SHOPPING

LYDIA'S MADE TO MEASURE SHOES

Custom-made and super chic! Reveal your most intimate shoe wishes to Lydia and she will transform them into the real thing. On average, it takes a week to make the footwear. *Mon/Tue, Thu/Fri 9am–7pm, Wed 9am–5pm, Sat 10am–2pm | 14 Tsami Street | lydias-shoes.com*

STOA PHYLACTOU

Get out of the heat. In this shady passage, you can take your time browsing in the small jewellery and souvenir shops. The restored shopping promenade ends at the café bar *Juego (daily 10am–midnight)* and its exit leads in the direction of the castle. *Between Agiou Andreas Street and Tzami Street*

SPORT & ACTIVITIES

Feel it's time for something completely different? How about freediving *(freedivingcyprus.com)* or stand-up paddling *(supclublimassol.com)* out on the gentle waves? For city tours, you can rent a bicycle at the *Next Bike station (nextbike.com.cy)*. *Fasouri Watermania (daily 10am–5pm, June–August until 6pm | admission 30 euros, children 17 euros | fasouri-watermania.com | F10)* a waterpark in Fasoúri, 6km from Limassol, sits in a beautiful green setting surrounded by citrus trees. Alongside the usual attractions, there is also a spa here.

INSIDER TIP **The fun bus**

In July and August, a shuttle bus *(return tickets 2.50 euros | stops marked on the waterpark's website)* operates from many of Limassol's hotels.

BEACHES

The advantages of the *city beach* are that there are bars and it's right in the centre. On the downside: the four-lane B1 runs right next to it. A more secluded and shadier spot is *Dasoudi Beach* which has its own woodland area. The beaches on the west side of the city are amazing, such as the long *Lady's Mile Beach* at the salt lake or the wide *Koúrion Beach*. *Governor's Beach (H10)* is also charming.

NIGHTLIFE

Dancing in the street! *Saripolou Square* is the party square. The clubs and bars around the old market hall merge into each other. Flitting from one place to the next was never this easy – it's just a few steps further before you reach the next party with atmosphere. The party goes on until 2am when the majority of bars and clubs close (closing time is the same during the week as at the weekend).

INSIDER TIP **Pull an all-nighter**

If you are still in the mood, head to *Retro Club (Odós Ifigénias 6)*, round the corner. On Fridays and Saturdays, it stays open until 5.30am.

GUABA BEACH BAR

Strap in – this club has become a destination in itself. Loud, manic and wild. It has been among the 50 best clubs in the world for years. Top tip: the Sunday parties with international DJs. *May–Oct daily 9pm–3am | Amathountos 7 | guababeachbar.com*

AROUND LIMASSOL

Rural buses are a cheap and cheerful option for getting to the mountains near Limassol (see p. 96, Tróodos). A day ticket costs 5 euros. You will find bus timetables and routes at *en.limassolbuses.com (Rural Routes)*.

1 ALASSA

15km / 20 mins from Limassol by car

When a church took the plunge …! To build the Koúris dam about 14km northwest of Limassol, Alassa village had to be resettled in 1985. Only the church remained. It was flooded and its tower is still visible today. It's a bizarre sight and great subject for a photo. *F9*

The sea and the horizon provide the backdrop at Koúrion's ancient theatre

2 CYPRUS WINE MUSEUM ★

10km / 20 mins from Limassol by car

Erími's wine museum is more than a building housing old objects and dry, sober explanations about their use. The excellent exhibition tells the history of winemaking on Cyprus, of course. But afterwards, you can partake in a tasting in the cellars. *Jámmas!* Cheers! *Daily 9am–5pm | admission incl. tasting 10 euros | cypruswinemuseum.com | 1.5 hrs | F10*

3 KOLÓSSI

15km / 25 mins from Limassol by car

Roaming through this fortified castle is slightly eerie. Everything still looks intact – rough stone walls, small windows, a single chimney for a vast hall. The crusaders must have frozen here! *Kolóssi Castle* once belonged to the order of the Knights of St John, who had their headquarters here until 1309. Their stone insignia is still visible on the walls today. Incidentally, Cyprus's most famous wine owes its name to the medieval knights. *Commandaría* wine is named after their administrative district, La Grande Commanderie. The knights not only made money from wine, but also sugarcane. The sugar was produced in the long hall, which at first sight looks like a ruined church. *April–Sept daily 8.30am–7.30pm; winter daily 8.30am–5pm | admission 2.50 euros | 1 hr | F10*

4 KOÚRION ★

15km / 25 mins from Limassol by car

Wow, what a view! From far below the rediscoverd city, the sea peeps through between the ruins and decorated columns. They knew how to handle a building project in antiquity. There are glorious *floor mosaics* to view in Koúrion as well as antique *thermal baths*. The water was heated for the baths of wealthy citizens. Now, take a seat in the top row of the *ancient open-air theatre*. Do you notice anything? In those days, no artificial scenery was required to perform plays. The landscape and colours of the sea and sky were enough to capture the imagination.

INSIDER TIP Greek drama

You can experience live performances of ancient plays *(greekdramafest.com)* here in the summer. *April–Sept daily 8.30am–7.30pm, winter daily 8.30am–5pm | admission 4.50 euros | 1 hr | E10*

5 PISSOÚRI

35km / 45 mins from Limassol by car

Up for a bit of nostalgia? Before the invention of the package holiday, people rented guest rooms – just like the ones here. In the village centre traditional rural life is still prominent. In the summer months, owners of the O'Vrakas and Symposio tavernas organise *Folklore Evenings* on Wednesdays and Fridays. It's not far for an excursion to *Platanisteia*, where you'll find the *Hambis Printmaking Museum (Wed–Sun 10am–1pm, 4–6pm; winter 3–5pm | free admission | hambisprintmaking center.org.cy)*. There, you can view erotic prints as well as the tools and machines that made them. Tours are also offered, along with workshops and various events. A must for bookworms! *D10*

6 ANÓGYRA (ANÓYIRA) ★

45km / 55 mins from Limassol by car

It's all organic here! This village and its inhabitants have focused on producing high-quality food and drinks of all kinds. Not only that, but they love showing it off (often for free)! You can try wine made by *Domain Nicolaides (Mon/Tue 10am–3pm, Wed–Sat 10am–5pm; winter until 4pm | FB: nikolaides.winery)*. Those with a sweet tooth can try carob bean *pasteli* sweets made at *To Paradosiako (farm shop daily 7am–7pm)*. At the *Ktima Stalies* dairy *(Mon–Sat 8am–5pm, Sun 10am–5pm | 1km outside the village)* you can watch the staff making halloumi and you can take flavoured oils home from the herb garden at *Anagyris Park & Restaurant (Tue–Sat 10am–4pm, Sun 10am–5pm)*.

INSIDER TIP From tree to (bath) tub

If you ask Marios, the owner, he will show you how to make soap from olive oil. You can learn more about carob in the *Carob Museum Mavros Chrysos (daily 9am–6pm, winter until 5pm)*. In *Oleastro Park*, just outside the village, you can visit the *Open Air Olive Museum (daily 10am–6pm | admission 3 euros | oleastro.com.cy)*, which has its own restaurant (of course!). *D9*

7 AKROTIRI ENVIRONMENTAL EDUCATION CENTRE

15km / 25 mins from Limassol by car

Inside, replicas of extinct and living animals from Cyprus can be seen in front of a reconstructed backdrop, while outside, on the salt lake, flamingos and other birds can be observed with binoculars. *Mon–Fri 7.30am–2pm, Sun 9am–1pm | free admission | Queen Elizabeth Street, Akrotiri | akrotirienvironment.com | 45 mins | F11*

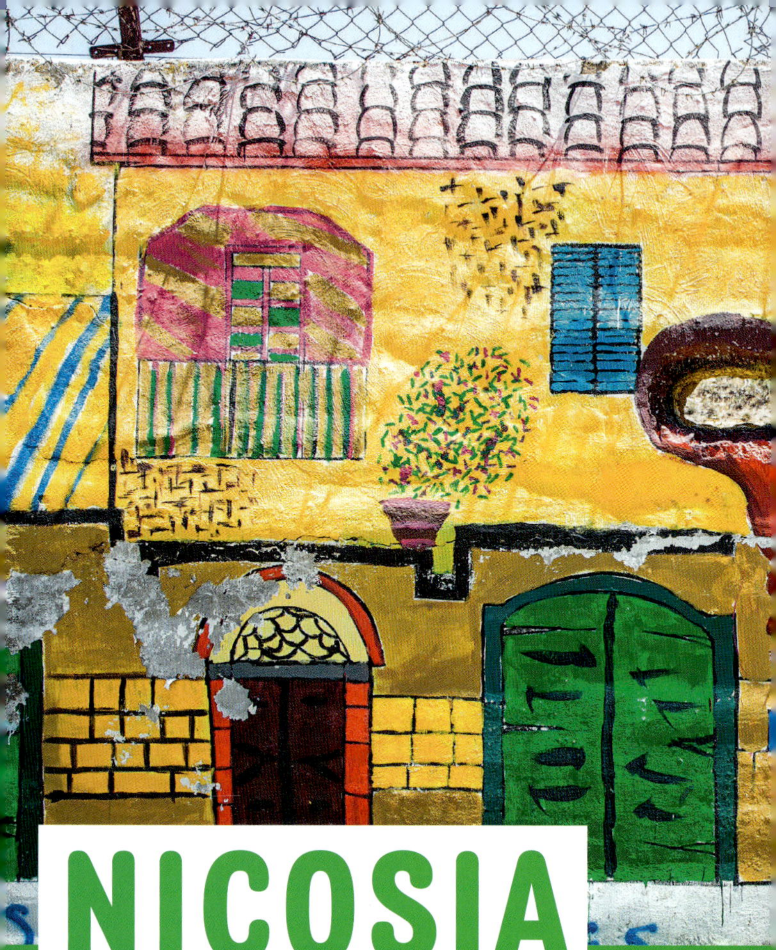

NICOSIA

A CAPITAL CITY WITH A SPLIT PERSONALITY

Nicosia is Cyprus's most exciting city – and a one-off! You'll come across barricades and ID checkpoints, and also find hipster bars next to shop displays from the 1970s. Some 240,000 people live in the south, while the north has a population of around 80,000. The capital has three names (Latin: Nicosia, Greek: Lefkosía, Turkish: Lefkoşa). Muezzin calls are audible five times a day and are joined by church bells on Sundays. These are just some of the everyday eccentricities of this divided capital city.

Colourful graffiti decorates the wall that divides Nicosia

Lídras Street – a pedestrianised shopping street in the city centre – ends abruptly at an unmanned checkpoint; a sign that the division here has lost much of its threatening edge. Once-forgotten alleys around the buffer zone have been transformed into idyllic corners with brightly coloured houses and flower boxes. On the Turkish-Cypriot side of the city, Bazaar Street is reminiscent of a bustling Middle Eastern shopping district.

NICOSIA

MARCO POLO HIGHLIGHTS

★ **BYZANTINE MUSEUM**
Stolen art back on display: 1,500 years old, hidden for 40 years, worth millions
➤ p. 69

★ **CENTRE OF VISUAL ARTS & RESEARCH**
Celebrating the glamour and fashions of the past, and commemorating the celebrated last Queen of Cyprus ➤ p. 70

★ **CYPRUS MUSEUM**
Erotic secrets carved in stone ➤ p. 72

★ **SELIMIYE MOSQUE/SOPHIA CATHEDRAL**
The muezzin calls the Muslim faithful to prayer from the same building where Cyprus's Christian kings were once crowned ➤ p. 73

Şehit Ecvet Yusuf
Polis Sokak
Adana Sokak
Ali Ruhi Sok
Pencizade
Mahmut Paşa
15 Home for Cooperation
Saixpir
Markou Drakou Avenue
Tanzimat Sokak
Müftü Ziyai Sokak
Rüstems Bookshop
Büyük Han
Caravanserais 18
E. Çetin Sokak
Beliğ Paşa Sokak
Yediler Sokak
Şht. Salahi Şevk et Sokak
Pafou
10 City walls
Kykkos Avenue
Liperti
Asinoú
Plateia Georgiou Poulia
Kalá Kathoúmer
Ledras Street
Lefkonos
Granikou
City Park 14
To Anamma
Cyprus Classic Motorcycle Museum 12
3 Bank of Cyprus Cultural Foundation
Palaion Patron Germanou Street
Arsinois
Lykourgou
Sophokleous
Mouseiou
Egypt Avenue
Rigenis
Omirou
Observatory 1
Sapfous
Aeschylus
13 Cyprus Museum
Avos Armenian Food
Chilonos
Fokionos
Ledras Street
2 Leventis Municipal Museum
Onasagorou
Solonos
Ippokratous
Kosti Palama Street
Omirou
Gladstonos
Vyronos
Diagorou
Anastasiou G.Leventi
Platía Eleftherías
Constantinou Paleologou
Riverland Bio Farm
Sofouli
11 Leventis Gallery
Stasinou
10 City walls

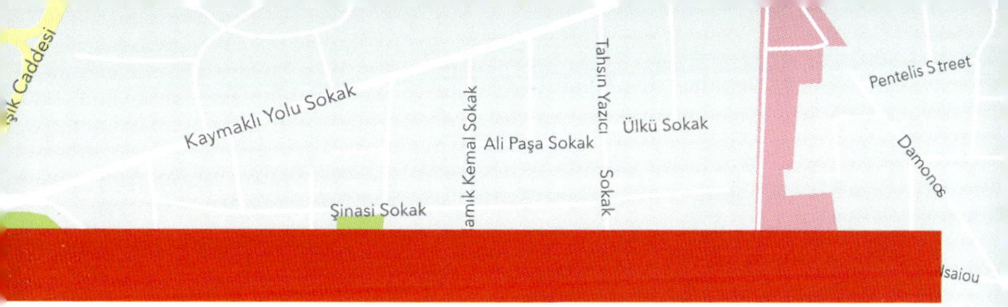

Kaymaklı Yolu Sokak
Şinasi Sokak
Ali Paşa Sokak
Ülkü Sokak
Tahsin Yazıcı Sokak
Pentelis Street
Damonos

★ BÜYÜK HAN

The caravanserais where camels used to recuperate after long journeys are now hubs for shopping and tourism ➤ p. 74

★ RIVERLAND BIO FARM

Stroke goats, watch cheese being made, go riding. Spend a day down on the farm ➤ p. 77

★ ASINOÚ

The 900-year-old wall paintings qualify this church as a UNESCO World Heritage Site ➤ p. 79

10 City walls
16 Selimiye Mosque/Sophia Cathedral ★
7 Bedestan
Market hall
Chrysaliniotissa Artists' Workshops
9 Centre of Visual Arts & Research ★
To Apomeron
Caraffa Bastione
8 Nicosia Municipal Arts Centre
6 Ethnographical Museum
7 Ágios Ioannis Cathedral
5
Byzantine Museum ★
4 Hadjiyorgákis Kornésios's House
Neverland Rockbar
Farmers' market
Fuzuli Sokak
Atilla Sokak
Ali Riza Sokak
Haydar Paşa Sokak
Karababa Sokak
Agiou Georgiou
Patroklou Street
Leof. Athinas
Christaki Christofidi
Raktivan
Lisippou
Pouliou kai Kapota Ave.
Uray Sokak
Baki Efenti
Ermou
Themistocleous
Lidinis
Manis
Pentadaktylou
Ymitou
Ammochostou Street
Ektoros
Polyviou
Aigeos Street
Aglaias
Thiseos
Tempon
Eptanissou
Alkiviadou
Thiseos Street
Solonos Michailidi
Apostolou Varnava
Isaakiou Komnhnoy Street
Attali
Peiraios
Agiou Dimitriou
Paionos
Korai Street
Leoforos Nikiforou Foka
Larnakos
Patriarchou Grigoriou
Bolonaki
Trikoupi Street
Agiou Antoniou
Elenis Palaiologou
Salaminos
Andrea Laskaratou
Areos Street
Onisilou
Athinon Street
Xenierou Street
Palaiologou
Archermou
Vitonos
Digeni Akrita
Xanthis
Xenierou
Constantinou
Simonidou Street
Poliklitou
Rikou
Meletiou
Metaksaki
Stasinou
200 m
219 yd

NICOSIA

(🕮 J5-6) **Nicosia's city boundaries extend into the Tróodos mountains. As a result, city bus tickets (5 euros) can take you as far as Kakopetria and back.**

SIGHTSEEING

1 OBSERVATORY

You don't need to fly a drone to get a panoramic view of the city. Simply look out of the windows of Shakolas Tower. In the observatory the telescopes have information boards that indicate what can be seen in various directions. *Daily June–Sept 10am–7pm, otherwise 10am–5pm | admission 2.50 euros | entrance at Arsinóis Street, southern Nicosia | 30 mins | 🕮 c5*

WHERE TO START ?

Old town: From the motorway, you head downhill directly into the old town – the original heart of Nicosia. Leave the car by the city walls in one of the large car parks. You'll thank yourself for this later when you see the rabbit warren of narrow streets and one-way roads that is the city centre. If you arrive on public transport, you will almost certainly also find yourself at the city walls – the main long-distance bus station, Platía Solomoú, is located there too. From the walls, grab a decent coffee from Ledra Street. After that, you will be ready to take on the world (or Nicosia at least)!

2 LEVENTIS MUNICIPAL MUSEUM

Now you've made it all the way here, it is probably worth developing an interest in Nicosia's thrilling 3,000-year history. Should that not be the case, how does a stellar jewellery collection sound? Necklaces, bracelets and rings with delicate ornaments in gold and silver, decorated scarf pins, elegant belt buckles – all exquisite items of jewellery used in the past. *Tue–Sun 10am–4.30pm | free admission | 3–5 Hippocrates Street, southern Nicosia | leventismuseum.org.cy | 1 hr | 🕮 c5*

3 BANK OF CYPRUS CULTURAL FOUNDATION

Does looking at ancient fragments of pottery bring out the bored teenager in you? Here you can put a replica of an old ceramic shard on a rotating disc and – voilà! – an intact vase appears on screen. The miracle of virtual reality! And just like that you can admire artefacts from 3,000 years ago through a different lens. And all of this is free … (ironically) even the ancient coin collection. The museum's gift shop has historical engravings from as little as 12 euros and replica ancient silver jewellery from 20 euros. *Daily 10am–7pm | free admission | 86–90 Phaneroménis Street, southern Nicosia | boccf.org | 1 hr | 🕮 c4*

INSIDER TIP
Superior souvenirs

4 HADJIYORGÁKIS KORNÉSIOS'S HOUSE

Celeb villa, 18th-century style! The homeowner was a certain Dragoman Kornésios, a VIP back in the day and a tax collector for the Sultan. No wonder he could afford golden ceilings. Perhaps he lined his own pockets too much – he was executed in 1809 in Istanbul. *Tue–Fri 8.30am–3.30pm, Sat 9.30am–4.30pm | free admission | Patriarch Gregórios Street, southern Nicosia | 1 hr | e5*

5 BYZANTINE MUSEUM ★

How permanent is art? Modern photo prints may fade after just a few years but the walls in this museum are decorated with mosaics that are 1,500 years old! Many of the exhibits here have spent much of their recent lives out of Cyprus, having been removed from churches, smuggled out of the country and hidden away. In the end, they were discovered, confiscated and stored for years in the exhibits vault of the Bavarian State Criminal Investigation Department before being handed back to Cyprus in 2013. Total value: 30 million euros. Not all the exhibits have such a compelling provenance but are no less beautiful for it, and the collection as a whole is a great introduction to the Cypriot Orthodox Church. You can download a free audio guide to the exhibition from the Ministry of Tourism's website. Just head to *visitcyprus.com*, select "Media" from the menu on the home page. Then search for "Byzantine Museum" with the filters "Culture and Religion" and "Audio Guides" selected. *Mon–Fri 9am–4.30pm, Sat 9am–1pm | admission 4 euros | Plateía Archipiskópou Kyprianoú, southern Nicosia | 1.5 hrs | e4*

INSIDER TIP
Listen and learn!

An audioguide will explain the religious art in the Byzantine Museum

6 ETHNOGRAPHICAL MUSEUM

Fortunately, this is not an antique shop but a museum. Otherwise, you would be tempted to go on a spree with the carved wooden chests and hand-painted ceramic bowls. The historic handicrafts and equipment would look as much at home in the ancient world as in a modern country house. *Tue–Fri 9.30am–4pm, Sat 9am–1pm | admission 2 euros | Archbishop Kiprianós Square, southern Nicosia | 30 mins | e4*

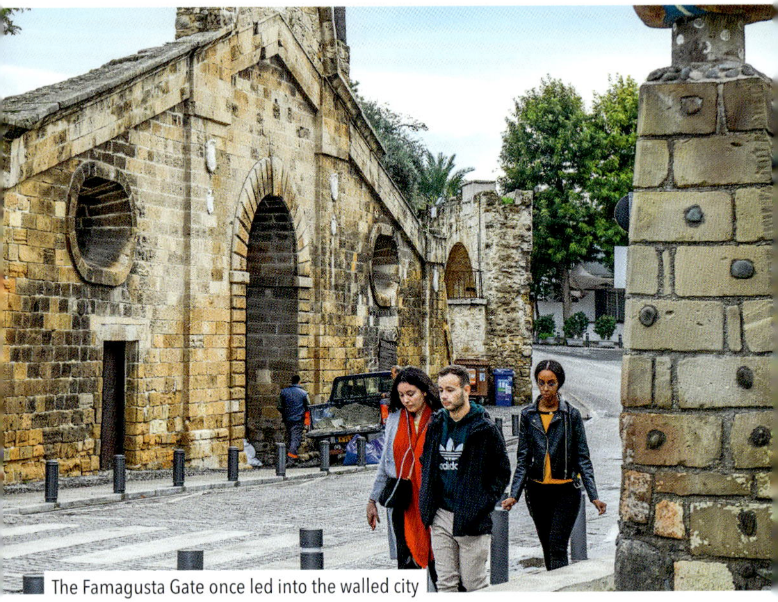

The Famagusta Gate once led into the walled city

7 ÁGIOS IOANNIS CATHEDRAL

Cute! This small 17th-century church is one of the smallest cathedrals in the world. Under the Ottomans it was not allowed to stand out in the city, so its grand decoration was saved for the interior. Look out for golden wood decorations, opulent chandeliers and brightly coloured frescos. Today, the Nicosians love the kitsch decor of the cathedral for their wedding ceremonies. *Mon–Fri 8am–noon and 2–4pm, Sat 9am–noon | free admission | Archbishop Kiprianós Square, southern Nicosia | 30 mins | e4*

8 NICOSIA MUNICIPAL ARTS CENTRE

What's that container hanging off the building? The flagship exhibit of this gallery in a former power station is not exactly meaningless art, but it makes a powerful statement. The numbers on the bottom of the container are projected onto the pavement at night; they belong to a never-ending series of UN resolutions on the Cyprus problem. These have still not delivered unification. If the modern art on display is not to your taste, there is still the *restaurant (Tue–Sat 11am–4.30pm, 6pm–1am, Sun 11am–4pm)* which has ample seating outside. *Tue–Sat 10am–9pm | free admission | Palias Ilektrikis 19, southern Nicosia | nimac.org.cy | 1 hr | e4*

9 CENTRE OF VISUAL ARTS & RESEARCH (CVAR) ★

Girl power already existed in Cyprus 500 years ago. In those days, Caterina Cornaro ruled the country as its undisputed sovereign. A whole room in the museum is devoted to her and the story of her life. Contemporary paintings depict the different stages of her reign in a kind of timeline: arrival in Cyprus, coronation, abdication. The paintings give a sense of a striking and powerful woman. The museum also houses a fascinating fashion collection with shoes, hats and traditional clothing from the last three centuries. A further collection of historical photos will give you such a good sense of Cyprus's past that you will hardly be able to tear yourself away. *Mon–Sat (winter Tue–Sat) 9.30am–5pm | admission 5 euros | 85 Ermoú Street, southern Nicosia | cvar.severis.org | (map) e3*

10 CITY WALLS

The circular city walls with their 11 bastions are so distinctive that they are used to symbolise the city on everything from its coat of arms to fridge magnets. The Venetian builders who constructed them about 450 years ago did modern residents a huge favour too, as the fortified bastions cannot be built up with new houses so a green belt remains around the old town. All three original city gates are still in use: *Famagusta Gate (map f4)* as an exhibition and events space, *Páfos Gate (map b4)* as a historic entrance, and *Kerýneia Gate (map c1)*, which houses northern Nicosia's tourist information office.

11 LEVENTIS GALLERY

Do you tend to avoid galleries on holiday because of the long queues? If so, Nicosia is your chance to enjoy great art. The Leventis collection is small, compact but perfectly formed. Without the crowds, you can enjoy works by Pierre-Auguste Renoir, Claude Monet, Marc Chagall and Giovanni Antonio Canal, or Canaletto. There is plenty to prick kids'

CROSSING BETWEEN NORTHERN AND SOUTHERN NICOSIA (CHECKPOINTS)

Lídras Street Checkpoint (map c4) is easy to get to but often overcrowded as this strange border crossing at the end of a shopping street in the old town is the most popular checkpoint in the city. Between 9am and noon, you can queue for up to half an hour.

Ledra Palace Checkpoint (map a2) on the edge of the old town is only ten minutes on foot from both city centres. It is never busy here and you can cross on foot or by bicycle.

Ágios Dométios Checkpoint (map 0) in the western part of the new town near the racecourse in southern Nicosia is the only checkpoint in Nicosia that you can cross by car.

Just outside the city, there is another checkpoint which takes you from Astromerítis in the south to Morfou (Güzelyurt) in the north.

All checkpoints are open round the clock.

interest too. Each floor has a "learning table" where they can play computer games based on the art around them. *Wed 10am–8pm, Tue–Sun 10am–5pm | admission 3 euros |5 AG Leventis Street | continue on Ledra Street beyond the city walls, southern Nicosia | leventisgallery.org | ⏲ 2 hrs | 🕮 b6*

12 CYPRUS CLASSIC MOTORCYCLE MUSEUM

The vintage motorcycles in this exhibition will certainly move any hard-core biker fans in your group with their beauty ... and even sceptics will find it hard to deny their aesthetic value. A mixture of chrome, paintwork and leather will whet the whole group's appetite to have a go riding one. Andreas, the owner of the collection, restored each one of the 150 bikes (which date from 1914 to 1983). His wife and sons are as mad about them as he is, and you're virtually guaranteed to meet one member of this enthusiastic family in the museum. *Mon–Fri 10am–5.30pm, Sat 10am–1pm | admission 5 euros | 44 Graníkou Street | cyclassicmotormuseum.wixsite.com/cyclassicmotormuseum | ⏲ 30 mins | 🕮 b4*

INSIDER TIP
Be a biker for a day

If motorbikes are your thing, the fun does not have to stop at the museum's door; *motolifetours.com* offers tours and daytrips on Harley Davidsons. You can either ride pillion or take the controls yourself. (Prices start at 260 euros).

13 CYPRUS MUSEUM ★

A frivolous piece of classic art is hidden in the Cyprus Museum. The pedestals in Room 5 reveal at the front the harmless face of Dionysos. But look at the back! The passionately intertwined couple depicted here bear witness to the extended festivities that were once held in honour of the god of wine. Indeed, this couple are not alone; a lot of the archaeological exhibits here are dedicated to love. Whether they are sculptures, jewellery or cult objects – the goddess of fertility appears in multiple forms.

Overall, be careful in this museum not to lose sight of its breadth for the sake of seeing its most famous exhibits (the marble statue of Aphrodite from Sóloi or the naked bronze statue of the Roman Emperor Septimius Severus). One small example is the exquisite vase decorated with a bird catching a fish. This motif, which is at least 2,500 years old, appears so modern that it could easily be used today to decorate ceramics or souvenirs. *Tue–Fri 8am–6pm, Sat 9am–5pm, Sun 10am–1pm | free admission | 1 Museum Street, southern Nicosia | ⏲ 2 hrs | 🕮 a–b5*

14 CITY PARK

If you've got hot feet from all the walking around, you can cool them in the fountains among palm trees and flowering bushes. On Sundays, however, it gets crowded here. Immigrants from India, Pakistan, Sri Lanka and other countries meet for a picnic, offer their cosmetic services *(eyebrow threading, 5 euros)* and sell home-made food.

The Selimye Mosque was built as a Gothic cathedral

INSIDER TIP
South Asian snacks

The dishes are mostly prepared at home then served from simple pots to hungry guests. It's well worth trying anything that takes your fancy! *Always freely accessible | entrances in Museum Street, Nechroú Street, Kinyra Street, southern Nicosia | a4*

15 HOME FOR COOPERATION

A cuppa in no man's land? There aren't many places in the world where you have that option. The café in the *H4C* is a rendezvous for artists and peace campaigners from both sides of the city. If you don't get involved in animated conversations while here, you only have yourself to blame. *Mon–Fri 9am–7pm, Sat 9am–4pm | Markou Drakou Street 28, behind the checkpoint at Ledra Palace Hotel | home4cooperation.info | a3*

16 SELIMIYE MOSQUE/SOPHIA CATHEDRAL ★

If you've never been inside a mosque, seize the opportunity to change that in a place of worship that not only has a deeply spiritual atmosphere but which also reflects much of Cyprus's contested history. Remember to take off your shoes and cover exposed shoulders with scarves (available at the entrance). On entering, don't be surprised if you feel as if you have walked into a Gothic church. This house of God was built as a coronation cathedral in the 13th century. When the Ottomans changed the church into a mosque, some time after 1571, they added two minarets to the roof. This change of religious function is clearly reflected in the stylised decoration of the mosque's interior. There is space for women to pray at the back of the main prayer room, while the men take up their positions further forward.

Tables and chairs have replaced camels and traders in Büyük Han

Freely accessible, except during prayer times | Arasta Sok, northern Nicosia | 15 mins | d3

17 BEDESTAN

You don't need magic mushrooms to fall into a trance. The dervishes of the Mevlevi order will do that by "whirling" in a circle. If you feel dizzy just watching, look up and admire the Gothic arches. Today's cultural centre was the former Church of St Nicholas, and under the Ottomans it was a market hall *(bedestan)*. *Performances Mon–Sat noon, 2pm, 3pm, 5pm | admission 7 euros | next to the Selimiye Mosque, northern Nicosia | 30 mins | d3*

18 CARAVANSERAIS

In the days when merchants entered the city on camels, they would recuperate from their journeys in the "caravanserais". Today art and kitsch are sold in what was once their sleeping quarters and, where animals were once tethered, there are now restaurant tables. The best-known of these former hostelries is ★ *Büyük Han* (The Great Inn, 1572). There are no prizes for guessing how the 17th-century *Kumarcilar Han*, or Gambler's Inn, got its name. *Closed Sun | entrances Asmaaltı Sokak and Kurtbaba Sokak, northern Nicosia | c3*

EATING & DRINKING

In southern Nicosia, you will find a cluster of cafés and tavernas in the old town triangle between Laikí Gitoniá *(c5)*, Lídras *(c4–5)* and Onasagorou Streets *(c4–5)*. It stretches to the Faneromeni Church *(📖 c4)*. There are more to be found around the Famagusta Gate. In northern Nicosia, the traditional restaurants and bars are concentrated around Büyük Han, while in Dereboyou Street *(📖 0)* there are restaurants and cafés popular among the locals.

AVOS ARMENIAN FOOD

This is *the* place in the city to go for *lahmacun* ("Turkish pizza"). It is tasty, cheap and so easy to eat that it won't end up down your shirt. It's ideal for a meal on the move or as an evening snack before the next party. *Mon–Thu 8am–11pm, Fri–Sun 8am–11.30pm | 20 Onasagorou Street, southern Nicosia | € | 📖 c5*

CARAFFA BASTIONE

The kind of setting money can buy: the terrace is surrounded by three arches of an old aqueduct. To drink you should try "Breakfast in Nicosia", a cocktail of gin, cointreau, fig jam and lemon juice. It's a knock-out! *Tue–Thu 7.30–11pm, Fri/Sat 7.30–11.30pm | 6 Athinas Av., southern Nicosia | tel. 22 73 00 25 | bastione.com.cy | €€€ | 📖 f4*

KALÁ KATHOÚMENA

The doyenne of all indie cafés in Nicosia has the much-loved charm of a place that has been popular for decades. It is a meeting point for the capital's artistic and alternative crowd, who gather over a glass of wine or a cup of coffee. No matter whether Távli pieces are being pushed around the tables or new projects are being debated, there's always a great atmosphere. *Daily 10am–11pm | 21 Nikokleous Street, can also be reached via Stoá Papadopoúlou, a side street off Lídras, southern Nicosia | € | 📖 c4*

RÜSTEMS BOOKSHOP

Time to go against everything your parents told you and read at the table! On the top floor of Rüstems Bookshop, the manager has set up a buzzy lunch spot. Surrounded by precious antiques from the British colonial period, she serves a few specials every day (there is no menu). You willingly put down your book when lentil salad or chicken with *molohiya* (a kind of spinach) is served. Once you have finished lunch, head into the beautiful, green courtyard with a coffee. The shop itself makes a great photo op thanks to its huge bookcases and stylish furniture. *Lunch Mon–Fri noon–2pm, courtyard café Mon–Sat 9am–6pm | Girne Caddesi | opposite Saray Hotel, northern Nicosia | FB: Tustem Kitabevi | € | 📖 c3*

INSIDER TIP
The art of reading

TO ANAMMA

Save money, Greek style! This mini taverna serves individual souvlaki kebabs. You can either order them plain (1.10 euros) or with bread and salad (from 2.10 euros). Seating is outside with views over the busy Ledra boulevard on one side and the restaurant's patio on the other. *Daily noon–11pm | Odós Lídras 89, southern Nicosia | tel. 22 21 02 00 | toanamma.com | € | 📖 c4*

Shady Lídras Street is a pleasant place to shop and relax

TO APOMERON

A great Cypriot breakfast and home-made cakes are the hallmarks of this lovely little café in the middle of the old town. There are tables in a covered alley, so it's comfortable here even in the hottest summer heat. *Mon, Thu/Fri, 10am–11pm, Wed 10am–midnight, Sat/Sun 9am–11pm | Odós Poliviou 24 southern Nicosia | € | (map) e3*

SHOPPING

Southern Nicosia's main shopping areas in the old town are *Odós Lídras* (with all your favourite fashion chains) and *Odós Onasgórou Street* (alternative shops). *Makários Avenue (map c6)* (expensive brands) is the best spot in the new town. You'll find plenty of souvenir shops in the historic district of *Laikí Gitoniá*. In northern Nicosia *Arasta Sok (map c–d3)* is the main shopping street of the Turkish-Cypriot old town.

CHRYSALINIOTISSA ARTISTS WORKSHOPS

Browsing among the small studios here is a joy! While the artists get on with their sculpting, carving or painting, you check the finished pieces for a suitable souvenir. *Mon–Fri 10am–6pm, Sat 10am–2pm | 2 Dimonaktos Street | southern Nicosia*

MARKETS

Snacking allowed! If you taste the fresh fruit at the farmers' market at Constanza Bastion by the city wall *(map d5–6) (Wed/Sat 6am–5pm)*, the stallholders won't raise an eyebrow. You will hear the market before you see it, with the traders loudly calling out their wares. If you don't know what to do with *kolokassi* (a root vegetable) or snails, then simply ask for a recipe.

In the restored market hall in the old town in northern Nicosia *(📖 d3) (Mon–Sat 8.30am–5.30pm)* alongside fruit and veg traders, you will also find plenty of souvenir shops.

SPORT & ACTIVITIES

SEGWAY STATION

In Prague, they are banned and in Berlin, you need a driver's licence to ride one. What are we talking about? Segways! But in Nicosia, anyone can have a go. There are tours through the old town, lasting two or three hours, with informative guides and a coffee break. *Daily 10.30am, 2.30pm, 7pm | 38 euros/2 hrs | 48 euros/3 hrs | registration tel. 22 76 37 36 | 77A Aischylou Street | segwaystationcyprus.com | 📖 d4*

WELLNESS

STEAM WELLNESS BATH

A hamam in summer? Yes, please! Even with temperatures outside around 40°C, the ultimate way to relax is to be immersed in warm water and recline on hot stone. In the southern part of the city, the old Ottoman hamam ☂ *Omeriye Hamam* on Plateía Tyllirías has been restored. *Tue–Sun 10am–8.30pm | hamamomerye.com | (📖 d4).*

NIGHTLIFE

NEVERLAND ROCKBAR

There's always time to rock out! A phrase to live by and one that takes on new significance in Nicosia. Just as its literary name implies, Neverland keeps going even when all the other bars and clubs are asleep. *Sun–Thu 8pm–2.30am, Fri/Sat 8pm–3.30am | Nikiforou Foka 1, southern Nicosia | 📖 e5*

AROUND NICOSIA

TAMASSÓS

20km / 45 mins from Nicosia by bus (no. 100)

Walking down the stone steps into the ancient *"Royal Tombs" (Mon–Fri 9.30am–5pm, winter 8.30am–4pm | admission 2.50 euros | Politikó | 20km southwest of Nicosia)* in Tamassós can bring out strange feelings in you. Rich residents of the region were laid to rest here 2,500 years ago. It's not clear whether they were in fact royalty, but entire houses were built for them below ground – complete with ceiling beams, door frames, false windows and doors. And we think you'll agree, that's pretty spooky. *📖 H7*

RIVERLAND BIO FARM ★

25km / 40 mins from Nicosia by car

Spend a day of your holiday down on the farm! Kids (and some adults too) can learn where milk, cheese and

AROUND NICOSIA
Zümrütköy-(Katokopia)
Yukarı Bostancı
Mammari
Alayköy
Nicosia
A9
Κοκκινοτριμιθιά
Kokkinotrimithia
Ακάκι
Akaki
Περιστερώνα
Peristerona
Στρόβολος
Strovolos
Latsia
CYPRUS
ΚΥΠΡΟΣ - KIBRIS
25 km, 40 mins (partly unsurfaced)
30km, 45 mins
Tseri
Nikitari
Αγία Μαρίνα
Ayia Marina
Psimolofou
A1
Asinoú
Mitsero
Tamassós
Politiko
Άγιος Γεώργιος
Ayios Georgios
Aes Ambelis Winery
Klirou
Kampia
Riverland Bio Farm
Ayia Varvara
Kannavia
Ayios Epiphanios
Καπέδες
Kapedes
Lagoudera
Fikárdou
5 km
3.11 mi

fresh eggs from. There is also plenty of opportunity to spend time stroking the animals or donning a helmet and taking the horses and donkeys for a ride. On top of that there is archery, climbing, canoeing and a range of other outdoor activities. Convinced yet? Well, there is an excellent café selling the farm's produce. *Daily 9am–7pm | admission free | riverland biofarm.com |* H7

FIKÁRDOU

30km / 45 mins from Nicosia by car (very windy mountain road)

This village has fewer residents than many flat shares. Only seven people permanently live here. Perhaps as a result, Fikárdou is an idyllic place (and one with listed status). Those who enter the basic-looking museum *(daily 9.30am–5pm, winter 8.30am–4pm | admission 2.50 euros)* will feel as though they have set Doc Brown's time machine to the year 1900 and that they should be met by deeply confused local residents in traditional dress when they leave. H7

AES AMBELIS WINERY

25km / 40 mins from Nicosia by car

Ever feel you've had enough of your job? Then ask George Tripatsas how to tackle things. The owner of the Aes Ambelis Winery is a former banker who has dedicated the last 25 years of his life to becoming one of the country's best vintners. His multi-award-winning Commandaria is a bestseller. *Tasting and sales daily 10am–4pm, tour of the cellar by registration | tel. 99 83 56 63 | Kaló Chorío Orinis | aesambelis.com |* H7

ASINOÚ ★

42km / 50 mins from Nicosia by car

It's hard to believe that this small church is a designated World Heritage Site. From the outside, it looks almost boring: stones, a shingle roof and not even a bell tower. However, it is hiding a wealth of treasures inside. Some of the brightly coloured wall frescoes have survived for 900 years.

The strange cladding of the church Panagia tis Asinoú protects the inside from the wind and weather. There are other examples of these cleverly constructed, vaulted, barn-style-roof churches in Tróodos, where nine other churches are on the UNESCO list. *Mon–Sat 9am–4pm, Sun 11am–4pm | free admission |* 🕮 *F7*

The plain exterior of Asinoú church conceals an impressive and colourful interior

PÁFOS

A HOME FOR A GODDESS

Feel the adrenalin kick on an adventure trip, explore lost cultures and relax in the evening by the harbour with a glass of wine – if the Páfos holiday package didn't already exist, it would have to be invented! In western Cyprus you may have to check your jaw is not permanently dropping.

Nature has done a great job on the Akámas peninsula: wilderness, precarious sandy slopes on steep mountains, a mysterious gorge and a perfect blue lagoon. Don't worry about your hire car, jeep

Aphrodite's Rock, near Páfos, is where the goddess is said to have emerged from the sea

safaris will take you on adventurous paths through the most inaccessible terrain. Those less interested in adventure can follow in the footsteps of the goddess of love – the pursuit, according to some, is an aphrodisiac in itself … And don't just look in the places where legend suggests she visited, but also among the magical ruins of her temple in Koúklia, where the ancients celebrated her cult in not entirely holy ways.

PÁFOS

Blue Lagoon
Akámas
8 Baths of Aphrodite (Loutrá tis Aphrodítis)
Akámas peninsula 7
Latsí 9
Νέο Χωριό
Neo Chorio
4 km
2.49 mi
Androlikou
Mesógeios Thálassa
(Mediterranean Sea)
6 Lára Bay
Δρούσια
Drousia
Pano Arodes
Avakas Gorge 5
Ágios Geórgios 4
Peyia
Coral Bay
Kissonerga
Lémba
Archaeological Park
Páfos Mosaics

MARCO POLO HIGHLIGHTS

★ **PÁFOS MOSAICS**
These amazing mosaics prove that Roman living rooms looked a bit more interesting than ours do today ➤ p. 84

★ **THE PLACE**
Learn how traditional crafts were made on the island. You can watch the artisans at work and buy the fruits of their labour as souvenirs ➤ p. 89

★ **APHRODITE'S ROCK**
This is where the goddess of beauty emerged from the waves. It is said that bathing here will keep you beautiful too ➤ p. 92

★ **AKÁMAS PENINSULA**
Get ready for adventure in the wilderness ➤ p. 93

★ **WINE ROUTE 1**
Beautiful mountain views and something to enjoy them with ➤ p. 94

Argaka
Pano Argaka
E704
10 Pólis
Πελαθούσα
Kinoussa
B7
Chrysochou
Steni
ΚΥΠΡΟΣ - KIBRIS
CYPRUS
Skoulli
35km, 50 mins
ritou Terra
Sarama
Pano
Akourdaleia
Simou
Yiolou
Lasa
Πάνω Παναγιά
Pano Panagia
Kathikas
B7
Tràkkos Donkey Farm
Agios Demetrianos
12 Wine Route 1
Statos
kourssos
Πολέμι
Polemi
Γαλαταριά
Galataria
Στρουμπί
Stroumpi
13 Baths of Adonis
Kili
Λετύμβου
Letymbou
Πενταλιά
Pentalia
Γάλα
Tala
Τσάδα
Tsada
Καλλέπεια
Kallepeia
B7
Αμαργέτη
Amargeti
Κελοκέδαρα
Kelokedara
Έμπα
Empa
Mesogi
Armou
Episkopi
The Place
Stavrokonou
25km, 45 mins
Konia
Páfos
p. 84
Νατά
Nata
Ayios Yeorgios
1 Geroskípou
Choletria
rbour
Agia Barbara
Αναρίτα
Anarita
Pano
Archimandrita
A6
La Playa
Αχέλεια
Achelia
Τίμη
Timi
Νικόκλεια
Nikoklia
Μανδριά
Mandria
2 Koúklia (Palaiá Páfos)
Alectora
15km, 30 mins
A6
Pissouri
3 Aphrodite's Rock

PÁFOS

(📖 B9) **The old town of Páfos (64,000 inhabitants) lives a double life: down in Káto Páfos, everything is designed around tourists. There are all-inclusive hotel districts, harbour tavernas and a street filled with bars. In the Archaeological Park, there are the ruins of high-society villas from ancient Roman times.**

The upper town, *Pano Páfos* – also called Ktíma – is where the genuine "Pafiti" live and hang out. The residents of Páfos are well known for their helpful attitude and friendliness. Páfos was European Capital of Culture in 2017 and the effects of the regeneration this led to are still evident – especially in Ktíma.

SIGHTSEEING

SIGHTSEEING BUSES

The red, double decker, "hop-on, hop-off" buses start in the car park by the harbour and take visitors to 11 major sights in the town. *Daily departures at 10am, 11am, noon, 1.30pm, 3pm and 4pm | 13.50 euros.*

City buses are a cheaper way to get around *(day tickets 5 euros, children under 12 go free | pafosbuses.com)*. The no. 611 takes you east of the centre towards Geroskípou Beach (and the waterpark), the no. 615 goes to Coral Bay in the west (and to the royal tombs). The nos. 610 and 618 commute between the lower part of Páfos and Ktíma. Tickets are valid across the whole Páfos district on the day of travel.

ARCHAEOLOGICAL PARK

Ooops! A farmer gets stuck ploughing his field and what does he find? Several brightly painted stones. He could have taken them with him and used them as coasters for his morning coffee. Fortunately, he didn't, and the archaeologists knew what to do. Since 1962, they have uncovered ★ *magnificent mosaic floors* under this erstwhile field. They mostly originate from the third and fourth centuries and belonged to rich Roman villas. Over the years the remains of an entire town have been revealed in the *Archaeological Park*, right beside the harbour. The sight of these images created with tiny stones never ceases to amaze. And they are not just beautiful – the "permanent carpets" inside the houses would serve as a pretty decent collection of ancient mythological tales. Even 1,500 years later, the images are still almost as vivid and beautiful as they would have been on the first day – that's not bad craftsmanship!

The Archaeological Park also includes an *open-air theatre (Odeon)*, which is still used for concerts, the remains of the *Saranda Kolonnes Fortress (Forty Columns)* and the *Royal Tombs* (see p.87). *April–Sept daily 8.30am–7.30pm; winter 8.30am–5pm | admission 4.50 euros | harbour | ⏲ 1.5 hrs.*

INSIDER TIP **Money saver!**

You can buy a day ticket for all the public museums and ancient sites in Southern Cyprus for 8.50 euros. Multi-day options are also available. For 17.50 euros,

The Romans preferred mosaics to carpets in their homes

you get unlimited access for three days 25 euros for seven days. You can buy the tickets at the admission desks in any museum and they are valid across the south of the island.

HARBOUR

The picture of disarmament: previously, the *Castle (April–Sept daily 8.30am–7.30pm, winter 8.30am–5pm | admission 2.50 euros | ⏲ 30 mins)* by the harbour was there to defend against enemies. Today, it serves as a concert venue and outdoor opera house. However, if you happen to be in Páfos on a day when there are no cultural events, it's worth making the short climb to the ramparts to enjoy the wonderful view.

The restaurants and tavernas along the quayside will try to tempt you in with special offers. In the end it doesn't really matter. Whichever one you choose – it's a wonderful spot with a great view of the moored boats.

FABRICA HILL

Away from the Archaeological Park, there is a another version of the historical heritage of Páfos to discover. To the northeast there is an area that contains an ancient quarry with caves, remains of a Hellenistic amphitheatre and other ruins, separated from the Archaeological Park by a busy road. For a long time Fabrica Hill was largely visited only by people coming across it by chance. However, after years of construction, an elevated steel walkway now leads directly to the site. Starting at the side exit of the Archaeological Park, the winding walkway stretches

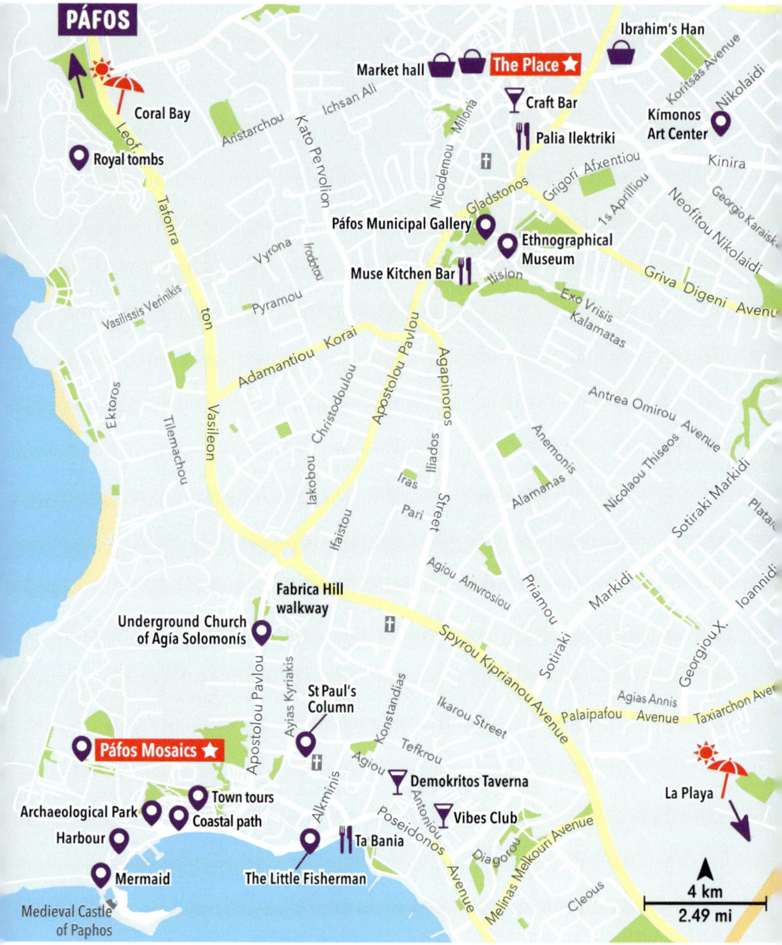

PÁFOS
Coral Bay
Royal tombs
Market hall
The Place
Ibrahim's Han
Craft Bar
Palia Ilektriki
Kímonos
Art Center
Páfos Municipal Gallery
Ethnographical
Museum
Muse Kitchen Bar
Fabrica Hill
walkway
Underground Church
of Agía Solomonís
St Paul's
Column
Páfos Mosaics
Town tours
Archaeological Park
Coastal path
Harbour
Mermaid
Medieval Castle
of Paphos
The Little Fisherman
Ta Bania
Demokritos Taverna
Vibes Club
La Playa
4 km
2.49 mi
Leof.
Tafonra
ton
Vasileon
Aristarchou
Ichsan Ali
Kato Pervolion
Nicodemou
Milona
Gladstonos
Grigori Afxentiou
1s Aprilliou
Koritsas Avenue
Nikolaidi
Kinira
Neofitou Nikolaidi
Griva Digeni Avenue
Exo Vrisis
Kalamatas
Vyrona
Irodotou
Pyramou
Vasilissis Verinikis
Adamantiou Korai
Apostolou Pavlou
Agapinoros
Christodoulou
Iakobou
Ektoros
Tilemachou
Antrea Omirou Avenue
Anemonis
Alamanas
Nicolaou Thiseos
Sotiraki Markidi
Iras
Iliados
Pari
Street
Ifaistou
Agiou Amvrosiou
Priamou
Markidi
Sotiraki
Georgiou X.
Ioannidi
Spyrou Kiprianou Avenue
Agias Annis
Palaipafou
Avenue
Taxiarchon Avenue
Ayias Kyriakis
Konstandias
Ikarou Street
Tefkrou
Agiou
Alkminis
Antoniou
Poseidonos
Avenue
Diagorou
Melinas Melkouri Avenue
Cleous

past a large mall to Fabrica Hill. From the top there are wonderful views. The entrance to the ruins is at the end of the bridge.

THE LITTLE FISHERMAN & MERMAID

What is the boy hiding behind his back? Everybody who passes the bronze sculpture, *The Little Fisherman* on the waterfront promenade feels the urge to look behind to find out. The artist Yiota Ioannidou knows how to make street art interactive. Her *Mermaid* behind the castle in the harbour – resting on the rocks – has become one of the most popular subjects for photos in town.

COASTAL WALK

Hat? Bottle of water? Shoes on? Let's go! Take the coastal path, which starts at the harbour, for 2.5km to the Royal Tombs. On the way, it passes the Archaeological Park and little stretches of beach where you can stop for a quick dip. If you are worried about walking in the heat, segways *(paphossegwaytour.com)* offer a more sedate option. There are several benches along the way where you can take a rest. They have been carefully located to maximise the view, so don't forget your camera.

INSIDER TIP
Snap away!

ROYAL TOMBS

Visit Páfos's most famous cemetery. Are you thinking of gravestones and plastic flowers? Forget it! This is a genuine necropolis – even 2,000 years ago, the rich and influential wanted beauty to last into eternity. Their family graves are arranged around an inner courtyard surrounded by columns. The burial chambers hewn into the rock have niches for burial objects. The relatives should not cross over empty-handed into the underworld.Incidentally, not a single monarch was laid to rest in the "royal tombs". The site's name is based on its majestic appearance. *April–Sept daily 8.30am–7.30pm, winter 8.30am–5pm | admission 2.50 euros | Tombs of the Kings Road,| Káto Páfos | 30 mins*

ST PAUL'S COLUMN

On Cyprus, free speech wasn't so popular back in the day. In the year 45, when St Paul came to the island to spread the word about the Christian faith, the Roman proconsul ordered him to be given 40 lashes. St Paul was allegedly tied to one of the columns that is still visible today on the site of the Panagía Chrissopolítissa church *(free admission). Káto Páfos | 30 mins*

UNDERGROUND AGÍA SOLOMONÍS CHURCH

It would be easy to completely miss this church. Not only does it sit on a busy road, but it is built into an underground catacomb complex. This complex is where the Christain

Making a wish at Agía Solomonís

convert St Solomoni took refuge when she was on the run from the Romans. Directly above the chapel at ground level, there is a tree covered in handkerchiefs, each of which contains a wish that believers hope the tree can grant. *Leofóros Apostólou Pávlou, Káto Páfos* | ⏲ *30 mins*

PÁFOS MUNICIPAL GALLERY

The courtyard is green and shady, the floorboards creak and at the entrance visitors are greeted like good friends. Visiting this gallery is like being taken on a tour of a friend's house. Pictures by local artists are displayed. Some are wonderful, others err towards the unsophisticated ... but collection and building together make for a charming ensemble. *Mon–Fri 9am–3pm, Sat 10am–1pm | free admission | 7 Gladstonos Street, Ktíma* | ⏲ *1 hr*

ETHNOGRAPHICAL MUSEUM

Is this a museum or is it that woman's house? When you look in through the museum's door, your eye is caught by an elderly lady seated in a chair, surrounded by household items from centuries past. Head on in though and you will hear stories about historic daily life here. The villa dates from the year 1894, while the furnishings have been compiled from different periods. *Mon–Sat 10am–5pm, Sun 11am–1pm | admission 3 euros | 1 Éxo Vrýssi Street, Ktíma | ethnographicalmuseum.com* | ⏲ *30 mins*

KIMONOS ART CENTER

Just watching will turn you into an artist here. Many of the most creative minds on Cyprus come together at the Kimonos. There are workshops and exhibitions on offer, and the atmosphere in the tiny studios is inspiring. Meet photographers, filmmakers, painters, comic illustrators and other visual artists. Join in, buy some art or just a cup of coffee and mingle with interesting people. *Mon–Fri 9am–12.30pm and 3–7pm, Sat 9am–1pm | 2 Kimonos Street, Páno Páfos | kimonosartcenter.com* | ⏲ *30 mins*

EATING & DRINKING

MUSE KITCHEN BAR

Let's start with the best thing about this restaurant: its view over the town is exceptional! At sunset, large groups of diners congregate on the small viewing platform to try and get the best shots. Thankfully the food is also of the very highest quality ... and that is served from early morning to late at night. The cocktails here are named after the muses in Greek mythology and it is fair to say that these goddesses have lent some divine inspiration to the recipes! Reservations necessary (especially in the evening). *Daily 9am–2am | Odós Andréa Ioánnou 16, Ktíma | tel. 26 94 19 51 | €€€*

PALIA ILEKTRIKI

Enjoy a break from the heat and noise: tucked away in the courtyard of the cultural centre in the old municipal utility company there is a friendly café and restaurant. While you're waiting for food (everything from T-bone steaks to lobster tails), you can cool your feet in the fountain. *Mon–Sat 10am–3pm and 5.30–10pm | Vladimerou Herakleous 8, Ktíma | tel. 26 22 21 57 | €*

TA BANIA

Our favourite spot! The Bania manages to be situated at the centre of the tourist quarter and still be cool and authentic. Minimalist design, by a becah (with changing facilities) and great music. *Daily 6pm–1am | Poseidonos Av. | tel. 26 94 15 58 | €€*

SHOPPING

IBRAHIM'S HAN

Within the warren of this old caravanserai, there is a network of tiny shops which specialise in local arts and crafts. There is also space for concerts and shows. *Daily 10am–6pm | Vasilissís Òlgas, Ktíma*

MARKET HALL ☂

In the renovated old market buildings, merchants now sell handicrafts and souvenirs. *Mon/Tue, Thu/Fri 9am–4.30pm; Wed, Sat 9am–2pm | Agorás Street, Ktíma*

THE PLACE ★

A little shopping, with a bit of entertainment and the opportunity to join in, this shop is an interesting mix of workshop and showroom. Creative handiwork and rustic products from the Páfos region are explained and are on sale. From 10am to noon, potters, carvers, whistle-makers and the rest show off what they can do. Some of them will let you have a go yourself.

People flock to the waterside tavernas on Páfos harbour

Mon/Tue, Thu/Fri 9am–4.30pm; Wed, Sat 9am–2pm | joining in 3–5 euros | 56 Kanari Street, Ktíma | theplace cyprus.com

SPORT & ACTIVITIES

Water sports are offered by all the big hotels; diving courses and excursions are also available, e.g. by *CyDive (cydive.com)*. In the area around Pólis, *Latchi Watersports Centre (latchiwater sportscentre.com)* offers all manner of sea-based activities from the harbour in Latsí! Páfos harbour is the point of departure for deep-sea fishing tours with *The Angler (theangler-paphos.com)*, as well as boat trips to *Coral Bay* and *Lára Bay*.

INSIDER TIP **Turtle watching**

Trips to go and observe turtles also start from Páfos harbour, setting off two hours before sunset in summer *(FB: Atlantis Turtle Watching Cruise)*. If you crave a bit more adrenalin on your holiday, *Aphrodite Waterpark (daily April–June 10.30am–5.30pm, July/Aug 10am–6pm, Sept/Oct 10am–5pm | admission 33 euros, children 3–11, 19 euros | aphroditewaterpark.com)* may be just the place for you and your kids!

The best golf courses are located near Páfos (see p. 34) Open-air yoga is becoming ever more popular, and *Kasia Yoga (paphosyoga.com)* offers rooftop yoga at sunrise or beach yoga *(10 euros/hr)*. *Ecologia Tours (wandern-zypern.de)* offers English-speaking nature tours around the area. Bicycles are available for rental in hotels and almost everywhere in Páfos, e.g. at *Mr Happy (mrhappybikerent.com)*, which offers guided day tours by bike, including to the turtle beach of Lára Bay, to the Aphrodite Rock and to the Tróodos Mountains (from 25 euros including bike, helmet and tour guide). The gentle mountain landscape around Páfos is a dream for horse riders (see p. 35)

BEACHES

Páfos has no town beach but its promenade has sunbeds and ladders that lead straight from the rock to the sea. Changing facilities are available, as is free WiFi. There are sandy beaches such as *La Playa* at Geroskípou, beneath the old lighthouse at the Odeon and, of course, at *Lára* (see p. 93) and *Coral* bays. The entire west coast has excellent sandy and pebble beaches.

WELLNESS

The enchanting green Milioú valley, 25km north of Páfos, is an ideal spot to retreat to if you are need of relaxation. And the *Agíi Anárgyri (aasparesort.com)* hotel has an excellent spa and wellness offering, with everything from sulphuric baths to yoga and oxygen-enriched drinks available for residents and non-residents alike.

NIGHTLIFE

CRAFT BAR

Chill out, chat and enjoy the live music. Alternative bar with retro student flat

While away a summer evening in the trendy bars around Páfos harbour

vibe. DJs play at the weekends. *Sun–Thu 7pm–1.30am, Fri/Sat 7pm–2am | 19 Alfredou tou Megalou Street, Ktíma | tel. 99 68 53 85 | FB: pafoscraft*

DEMOKRITOS TAVERNA

Party in retro style: as Cypriot as it gets … since 1971. The advertising slogan says it all: "Best Meals – Best Shows". *Daily 5pm–midnight | 1 Dionysou Street/Ágios Antónios ("Bar Street"), Káto Páfos | demokritostaverna.com | €*

VIBES CLUB

The ultimate place to be in Páfos with top-notch DJs and a maximum fun factor. *Daily from 1am | 25 Ágios Antónios ("Bar Street"), Káto Páfos*

AROUND PÁFOS

1 GEROSKÍPOU

6km / 15 mins from Páfos by car

What a sweet sight! *Lukúmia* from *Aphrodite Delights (Showroom Mon–Fri 7am–4pm | 2 Kantarénas Street/ Agapínoros Street | aphroditedelights.com)* is famous. The fruit jelly (flavours from rose to coconut) has been made and sold in Geroskípou since 1895.

Another attraction is the *Folklore Museum (April–Sept daily 9.30am–5pm; winter 8.30am–4pm | free admission)*, which explains how silkworms were bred and silk was spun in the village until World War II. *B9*

Avakas Gorge is a wild and mysterious place

2 KOÚKLIA (PALAIÁ PÁFOS)

18km / 30 mins from Páfos by car

This spot to the east of Páfos was once world famous. When Cyprus was still called Kypros, this was the site of the most important temple of Aphrodite. Find a spot in the middle of the ruins and close your eyes. Can you sense the hustle and bustle of all the pilgrims bringing a sacrifice to the goddess of love? Can you hear the fluttering of the white doves that fly through the open inner courtyard of the temple?

The black, gleaming stone that stood at the centre of the temple now stands intact in the *Museum (daily 8.30am–7.30pm; winter 8.30am–5pm | admission 4.50 euros)*. The cult of Aphrodite was – even by modern standards – on the more hedonisitic end of the religious scale (for more information, read the graphic novel mentioned on p.142).

The museum has many more objects to admire, such as a sarcophagus from the classical period that displays painted reliefs on all sides. One story depicted is unique in that it shows how Odysseus and his three companions strapped themselves to the underbellies of rams to escape the Cyclops Polyphemus. *C10*

3 APHRODITE'S ROCK ★

25km / 45mins from Páfos (bus 631 via Koúklia)

It happened here. This is the spot where the goddess of love is supposed to have emerged from the sea. And why not? The coastline with its sheer rock faces has the elegance of a goddess. If you swim round the rock three times, you are said to receive eternal beauty, youth and grace. However, the beach is very rocky here so be careful getting in and out of the water – especially if you want to look like Aphrodite in a photo!

INSIDER TIP **Eternal love with a guarantee**

It is said that if you write the name of your beloved on a flat stone from the beach here and then slot it into a crevice on the cliffs, the two of you will enjoy love forever. You never know ...Cypriots call the cliffs here, *Pétra tou Romioú* (The Stone of the Greeks) after Digenís

Akrítas, a Byzantine hero who is said to have held the Saracens at bay here. *C–D10*

4 ÁGIOS GEÓRGIOS

20km / 35 mins from Páfos by car

The church on the sea at Pégeia is an attractive spot and makes for a great stop if you are passing. On the flat plain, model-building freaks give their aircraft free rein, while far below are white rock formations and sea caves for climbing and swimming. The island opposite is only occupied by seagulls. Five hundred metres below the village, next to the sheltered fishing harbour, there is a small sandy beach with deckchairs for hire. The rocky coast is a popular place for walks. *A8*

5 AVAKAS GORGE

22km / 30 mins from Páfos by car

You won't be able to stop yourself from emitting a "wow" when you see the view here. It is truly spectacular. The hike through the gorge is one of the best (and most adventurous) things you can do on the island. The gorge itself – which sits on the Akámas peninsula – is just 4m across but its steep rock faces soar up to a height of 30m. You hike along the riverbed of the Avgas, navigating shingle and boulders. Sunlight rarely reaches the ground here, so it is shady and green even in summer. The route is about 1.2km long. On the return section, you can walk around the gorge, although this makes the route 10km longer. *B8*

6 LÁRA BAY

25km / 30 mins from Páfos by car

A *Turtle Conservation Station* has existed on Lára Bay on the west coast of the Akámas peninsula since 1978. Employees and volunteers help make sure that the thousands of baby loggerhead sea turtles and green sea turtles hatching from their sun-warmed eggs make it safely into the sea. The egg-laying and hatching period runs from June to September. *A7*

7 AKÁMAS PENINSULA ★

35km / 30 mins from Páfos by car

Untouched wilderness as far as they eye can see. The Akámas peninsula – with its forests, rock formation and special coastline – has protected status as a National Forest Park. There are no hotels, and only a few paved roads. So, you must either hike (find routes at *visitcyprus.com*) or book one of the (not so eco-friendly) jeep safaris that are offered on every street corner in Páfos. From *Latsí*, boat tours depart to the enchanting *Blue Lagoon*. *A6–7*

8 BATHS OF APHRODITE (LOUTRÁ TIS APHRODÍTIS)

43km / 30 mins from Páfos by car

Den of ancient iniquity! In this grotto, Aphrodite and her lover Adonis are said to have enjoyed a tryst. After a walk through the small Botanical Garden and over a shady path, you will find yourself looking at a tiny pond that is fed by a spring in a rocky grotto. A fig tree overshadows it, ferns and flowers line the rocky riverbank. Try to arrive early morning or in the evening to avoid the groups of visitors. The place's magic only really works if you are here alone. *Freely accessible during the daytime | A-B6*

9 LATSÍ

38km / 50 mins from Páfos by car

How about chartering a yacht and leaving to sail around the world? Looking out over Chrysochou Bay from the harbour in Latsí you will long for the open seas. We can all dream but for the time being why not join a fishing or bathing trip on a tourist boat? Tour offers are displayed on the quayside. You will find the beach beyond the harbour and its fish tavernas. If you need a quiet place to retreat to nearby, stop at *Yialos Beach Bar (Mon, Wed–Fri 11am–11pm, Sat/Sun 11am–midnight | between the harbour and the exit to the Baths of Aphrodite | FB: yialosbeach | €)*. Tables are set in the gap between the fields and the sandy beach, offering souvlaki, wine and an unhindered view of the bay – what else could you possibly need? *B7*

10 PÓLIS

35km / 50 mins from Páfos by car

If you are after a party resort Pólis is probably not for you. It is quite happy to leave the loud music and dancing to the metro-Pólis-es elsewhere on the island. However, you'll find the best atmosphere in the evenings in the small pedestrian zone between the pubs and bars. Holidaymakers here are likely to enjoy bicycle tours, relaxing on the beach and hiking excursions in Akámas. The local highlights are out in the wild, although the exhibits in the *Archaeological Museum (Mon–Fri 8.30am–4pm, Sat 9am–3pm | free admission | 26 Markaríou Street)* prove that a flourishing city kingdom once existed here.

One institution is *Arsinoe* fish taverna *(Mon–Sat 6.30am–11pm | Griva Digeni Street 3 | tel. 26 32 15 90 | €€)*. However, the cosiest place to sit and chill out is in the *Art Café (Mon–Sat 10am–4.30pm | Georgiou Street 1 | Pavlou | tel. 99 55 51 93 | €)*. It is run by a German woman and her homely cakes are not only delicious but also a tiny taste of northern Europe for those tiring of Cypriot cuisine. She also has a wealth knowledge about the island. *B7*

INSIDER TIP **Black Forest Gâteau**

11 LÉMBA

6km / 50 mins from Páfos by car

Who on earth would install a loo in the garden wall? Modern artists, of course! From the outside, the *Cyprus College of Art (garden freely accessible)* is an extremely striking building. The inner courtyard is even more intriguing. Generations of creative individuals have left their (occasionally unhinged) mark on the site. The free thinker who founded the college was Stass Paraskos. He was an ingenious painter who, in the 1960s, was one of the last artists to be prosecuted for obscenity in the UK. *B9*

12 WINE ROUTE 1 ★

A tip for wine connoisseurs/boozers! Simply follow the signs for *Wine*

Route 1 (red wine-coloured signs between Páfos and Polis) and you cannot fail to have a great day out. Pass through beautiful countryside with stops at several of the best wineries in the country: *Fikardos Winery (Mesógi | 🕮 B9)*, *Kamanterena Winery (Stroumpi | 🕮 B8)* and both wineries in Káthikas *(🕮 B8)*: *Vasilikon Winery* and *Sterna Winery*. The *Cyprus Tourism Organisation (visitcyprus.com)* has brochures on all the wine routes.

13 BATHS OF ADONIS

Ever thought about creating your own tourist destination? One way to do it is to build a huge statue to a Greek god beside a relatively unspectacular waterfall. But the fun doesn't start there. The path to the waterfall leads past erotic sculptures and through a building with old furniture (aka the museum). One self-built attraction follows the next. The owner calls this the *Baths of Adonis* ... However, the natural pool by the waterfall really is wonderful. Bathing and jumping are allowed. You can spend a few hours here with a picnic (snacks and drinks also available on site). Not only is it a genuinely nice way to spend an afternoon, but the only way to make the admission price worthwhile. *Daily 9am–6pm | admission 10 euros | drive off the road between Tála and Koíli | FB: Adonis Baths Waterfalls | 🕮 B8*

14 TRÁKKOS DONKEY FARM

25km / 30 mins from Páfos by car

This roadside farm is just before Káthikas. There are 80 donkeys here. Riding them costs 20 euros for an hour. In this time, the child on board can be switched as much as you like. *Daily 9am–6pm | tel. 99 68 01 99 | 🕮 B8*

FOR HIRE
WATERSPORTS CENTRE

Take a boat trip from Latsi harbour

TRÓODOS

PRETTY VILLAGES IN THE COOL MOUNTAINS

Do you know what luxury is? To sit in a shady mountain village in the baking summer heat, admiring the view of the majestic summits and feeling a cool mountain breeze. The Tróodos mountains are like a welcome air-conditioning system for the overheated island. And, on top of that, a new discovery for travellers is round every corner.

Once upon a time, only the wealthy could afford this refreshing climate. Film stars and royalty spent their summers in sophisticated

Ómodos is a picture-perfect village, with one of the most beautiful squares in Cyprus

mountain hotels here. Today, it is wine and wilderness that tempts tourists up to the mountains and away from the beach. The villages in this region were once sleepily hidden away, far from the big cities; today many of them have developed into lively places which offer visitors beautiful scenery – for sure – but also plenty of activities. Nonetheless, it is still hard to beat a day relaxing with the locals in a village *kafeníon*.

TRÓODOS

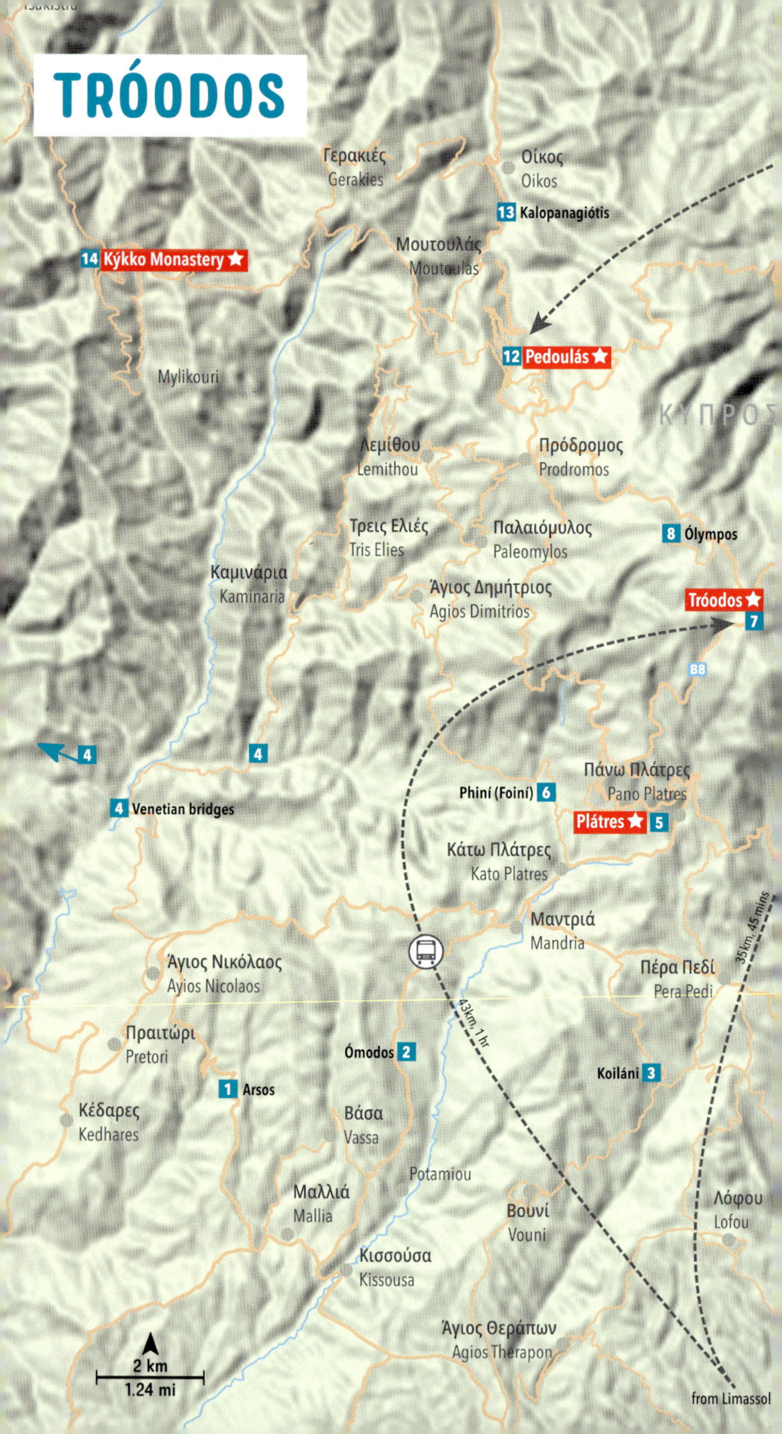

Γερακιές
Gerakies
Οίκος
Oikos
13 Kalopanagiótis
Μουτουλάς
Moutoulas
14 Kýkko Monastery ★
12 Pedoulás ★
Mylikouri
ΚΥΠΡΟΣ
Λεμίθου
Lemithou
Πρόδρομος
Prodromos
Τρεις Ελιές
Tris Elies
Παλαιόμυλος
Paleomylos
8 Ólympos
Καμινάρια
Kaminaria
Άγιος Δημήτριος
Agios Dimitrios
Tróodos ★ 7
B8
4
4
4 Venetian bridges
Πάνω Πλάτρες
Pano Platres
Phiní (Foiní) 6
Plátres ★ 5
Κάτω Πλάτρες
Kato Platres
Μαντριά
Mandria
35km, 45 mins
Άγιος Νικόλαος
Ayios Nicolaos
Πέρα Πεδί
Pera Pedi
43km, 1 hr
Πραιτώρι
Pretori
Ómodos 2
Koiláni 3
1 Arsos
Κέδαρες
Kedhares
Βάσα
Vassa
Potamiou
Μαλλιά
Mallia
Βουνί
Vouni
Λόφου
Lofou
Κισσούσα
Kissousa
Άγιος Θεράπων
Agios Therapon
2 km
1.24 mi
from Limassol

Καλλιάνα
Kalliana
B9
from Nicosia
70km, 1½ hrs
Γαλάτα
Galata
11 Kakopetriá
Κούρδαλι
Kourdali
Kannavia
Σπήλια
Spilia
Saranti
Lagoudera
55km, 1 hr 10 mins
KIBRIS
CYPRUS
B9
Χανδριά
Chandria
Alithinou
Κάρβουνα
Karvounas
Polystipos
Tróodos Geopark ★
Agridia
Alona
9 Páno Amíantos
Αμίαντος
Amiantos
Dymes
10 Agrós ★
Ποταμίτισσα
Πελένδρι
Pelendri
Kato Mylos
Ayios Ioannis
Μονιάτης
Moniatis
B8
Σαΐττάς
Saittas
Ζωοπηγή
Zoopigi
Άγιος Μάμας
Απεσιά
Apesia
Apsiou

MARCO POLO HIGHLIGHTS

★ **PLÁTRES**
A waterfall and a chocolate shop – everything you need for a perfect holiday ➤ p.101

★ **TRÓODOS**
Explore Cyprus's heights on foot ➤ p. 102

★ **TRÓODOS GEOPARK**
Where the mountains reveal their secrets ➤ p. 102

★ **AGRÓS**
This rosy village shows how to turn perfect petals into pretty products ➤ p. 103

★ **PEDOULÁS**
Step into a picture book in the tiny church of Ágios Michaíl ➤ p. 104

★ **KÝKKO MONASTERY**
Who says that monks have to be poor? This monastery got rich from an icon said to bring rain ➤ p. 105

SIGHTSEEING

It is easier to get to some villages from Limassol and to some from Nicosia. As a result, we have grouped the villages by the best point of departure. No matter which city you set off from, tickets that should get you all the way into the villages beyond the big towns and into the Troodos mountains cost 5 euros.

1 ARSOS

The stroll through the backstreets to the village square is enchanting. From quaint cottages to stately buildings, everything has been attractively restored. The village's history is explored in the *Folklore Museum (key in the coffee house on the village square)*. The shop at the *Kallena Botanic Garden (Mon–Fri 8am–6pm | FB: Kallena Arsos Botanic Garden)* sells organic products (tea, wine, syrup). On request, guided tours are available of the garden and distillery. *E8*

2 ÓMODOS

Any tourist who expresses an interest in visiting a wine village will be brought here. Fortunately, it won't disappoint. The large, paved Platía, with its many cafés, is one of Cyprus's most attractive village squares. If you want to try something typical, then buy an *arkatena* from the local baker. These circular pastries taste slightly sweet and – alongside the wine – make this village a destination for legal, addictive substances! At the heart of Ómodos is *Stavrós Monastery*. The church houses the skull and relic of the apostle Philip as well as (allegedly genuine!) splinters from the cross and remains of the ropes used to tie Christ.

INSIDER TIP **Rings of joy**

The main street is filled with souvenir shops but there is also a medieval wine press *Línos (open daytime | free admission)*. Once you understand the process, head next door to enjoy some tasting. *E8*

3 KOILÁNI

The village looks as if it has grown out of the surrounding vineyards. To some extent this is true – it is one of Cyprus's oldest wine villages and hosts the most traditional wine festival, the *Afamia Grape Festival (early Oct)*. Two of the best wineries are located here: vintner Sophokles Vlassides produces top-quality wines. The hypermodern architecture of his *Winery (Mon–Sat 11am–4pm | vlassideswinery.com)*, which looks out over the vineyards, is proof that new establishments can also hold their own within the wine-growing tradition. In the idyllic small wine cellar *Ayia Mavri (Mon–Fri 10am–4.30pm, Sat/Sun 11am–4.30pm)* you should try the white Muscat that has been awarded multiple gold medals over the years. Only a few bottles of this unusual wine are produced, so it is best to ask at the beginning of the tasting if you want to try it. Sweet with chilli notes, it is experimental but, in our opinion, extremely delicious. See if you agree! *E8*

INSIDER TIP **Bold flavours!**

4 VENETIAN BRIDGES

If there were only one of these bridges, it would be worth visiting for its magical forest setting. With three, they become a holiday must! The Venetian bridges along the rivers Xeros and Diarizos date back to the 16th century. Even in high summer, you can find a cool spot in the valley by the babbling water. Tip: take a blanket, snacks and cool white wine with you for a picnic.

Kelefou Bridge is above the village Ágios Nikólaos; *Roudia Bridge*, to the east, is near the deserted village of Vretsiá; while *Elia Bridge* is further north, near Kaminária. They are well signposted. *D-E8*

Ómodos: pick up handmade souvenirs here

5 PLÁTRES ★

Two villages for the price of one: Plátres is divided into Páno (upper) and Káto (lower) districts. And they both make for an idyllic stop on any trip to the Tróodos mountains. At an altitude of 1,100m, the temperatures are pleasant, and there are plenty of hotels and tavernas.

There are also two waterfalls nearby. The *Caledonia Falls* are reached along a *Nature Trail* that follows a wild stream through enchanting countryside. It is a walk that children might enjoy too (despite being three hours long). They can play pooh sticks and mess around in the streams – or even take a quick dip. The *Milomeri Waterfall*, on the other hand, is only a matter of a few steps from the car park.

The excellent *Lambouri Winery (Mon–Fri 10am–6pm, Sat/Sun 10am–8pm | lambouri.com)* is conveniently situated in the lower village of Káto Plátres. On the main street, *Psilo Dendro* serves fresh trout from its own farm *(Fri–Tue 10am–6pm | tel. 25 81 31 31 | FB: psilodendro | €)*. The *chocolate shop (Fri–Tue 10am–6pm | 6 Makaríou III Street | FB: cyprus chocolates)* offers pralines with distinctive Cypriot flavours: Zivania cream, walnut *palouze* or Aphrodite cream. Guided tours and workshops are also available.

If chocolate addiction is becoming a worry (for you or your kids), then the perfect antidote could be a trip to *Sparti Park (variable opening hours, check website | on the road from Káto to Páno Plátres | admission: adults from 50 euros, children from 25 euros (dependent on which route you choose) | spartipark.com)*. You will navigate tricky rope bridges, steep abseils and plenty of trees. By the end even the most grown-up adult will have fully reverted to childhood. *E8*

6 FOÍNI (PHÍNI)

The main reason to visit Foíni is the *Pottery Museum (enquire in the coffee house, if closed | free admission | signposted on the village street)*. The museum mainly explains Foíní's place as the most important village on the island for ceramics. The place is also known for its *loukoumia*. You can get the sweets fresh from *Ourania Pissourou (from 3 euros per pack | on the outskirts of town | FB: ourania.delights)*. *E8*

7 TRÓODOS ★

This village is a curiosity. Nobody lives here, and yet it is constantly overcrowded. The countryside, hotels, taverns, kiosks and shops have been enough to make it a tourist magnet. If you are in need of some healthy snacks, you can do a lot worse than *Cyprus Nuts*, who have a stand in central Tróodos. The wide variety of nuts are served salted, candied or roasted (with herbs and spices). They also have a large selection of dried fruit, with everything from cherries to pomelo. If you are travelling light, you can order more from their website, *cyprusnutsonline.com*.

INSIDER TIP
Cracking nuts

In winter Tróodos is the point of departure for skiers heading to Ólympos, and in summer walkers arrive to enjoy the hiking trails in the vicinity. Everyone else arrives for lunch, and an afternoon stroll along the nearby forest paths. There is no better place to start a walk than at *Tróodos Visitor Centre (April/May Mon–Sat 9am–2.30pm, Sun 10am–4pm; June–Aug Mon–Fri 9am–2.30pm, Sat/Sun 10am–4pm; Sept/Oct Mon–Fri, Sun 10am–4pm, Nov–March Mon–Fri 9am–2.30pm | admission 1 euro)* where guests can learn everything there is to know about these mountains. *E8*

8 ÓLYMPOS

This is peak Cyprus! At an altitude of 1,951m, Ólympos is the highest point on the island. On its slopes, you can hike, picnic and *ski (drag lifts 9am–4pm | skilift pass from 15 euros/day | snow from Dec to March | cyprusski.com/webcam)*. The only thing you can't do is climb up to the summit itself which is used for military purposes. The British radar station looks like a giant-size golf ball – a slightly threatening tourist sight but one that makes a great photo. *E8*

9 PANO AMIANTOS

If the mountains in Tróodos could speak, they would relate how the island of Cyprus was born from the ancient Tethys Sea. It sounds like the start of a Greek myth, but it is in fact correct. At the Visitor Centre in the ★ *Tróodos Geopark (Tue–Sun 9am–4pm | admission 3 euros)*, a fascinating exhibition tells the geological history of the mountains in such a way that you will never find rocks or stones boring again. Asbestos was mined here for many years; the mine is now closed and its old site is being reforested to transform it into a small natural park. Turning this barren landscape into a green oasis was a huge job that is described at the *Visitor Centre* in the *Botanical Garden (Mon–Fri 9am–2pm, park accessible anytime | free admission).*

Keep walking 1km down the road to reach the babbling *Golden Spring* (Chrysovrysi), which for many years after 1910 served as the main water source for the miners here. On a hot summer's day, you can't beat water from a mountain spring if you are in need of refreshment and this is no exception. Many Cypriots come up to the mountains with big water barrels and stock up for weeks at a time. If you want to join them, you will find this natural nectar in dozens of wells and springs throughout the mountains. So cup your hands or bring a bottle and do as the Cypriots do.

Nearby, in the *Amiandos Gardens Restaurant (Mon–Sat noon–9pm, Sun noon–5pm | FB: Amiandos Gardens Restaurant* | €) you can enjoy the best Cypriot cuisine. F8

Tróodos is not just a summertime destination

10 AGRÓS ★

If, when you get home, you look back on your trip to the high-altitude mountain village of Agrós with particular nostalgia, it might be because your glasses picked up a particular tint while there ... In the *Rose Factory (Mon–Fri 8.30am–5pm, Sat 9am–5pm, Sun 10am–5pm | 12 Triantafillou Street | venus-rose.com)* you can learn about how cosmetics are produced from fragrant rose petals. The small family factory demonstrates how it processes the roses and its shop sells everything from rose water and liqueur to aftershave.

INSIDER TIP Heavenly harvest

Those who are interested can help out with the harvest in April/May *(tel. 25 52 18 93)*. You will have to get up early and wear clothes that cover your arms and legs (because of the bees).

For something less sweet, try a visit to *Kafkália Butchers (Mon–Fri 8am–6pm, Sat/Sun 10am–1pm and 3–6pm | Kyriako Poitou Street 36| kafkalia.com)*, although vegetarians will want to give it a wide berth. The traditional

The overwhelming wealth of Kýkko Monastery is due to a miracle-working icon of the Virgin Mary

factory produces snacks like *lountza* (smoked pork fillet), *loukanika* (smoked pork sausages) and *pastourmas* (sun-dried beef sausage). Everything is explained in the shop and can be sampled together with wine and Zivania. F8

11 KAKOPETRIÁ

In English, the name of this village means "slanted rock" – and anybody who has ever tried build a house on the hard ground here will know why. For many city dwellers, Kakopetriá is known as a popular mountain village with a historic centre dating from the 18th and 19th centuries, the fast-flowing Kargotis and Garillis rivers, lush greenery and many tavernas. There is also a quaint old water mill next to *The Mill* hotel.

If you've come by a car, don't miss a detour to the church *Ágios Nikólaos tis Stégis (Tue–Sat 9am–4pm, Sun 11am–4pm | free admission)* about 5km outside Kakopetriá. From the outside, it looks like a large farmhouse, but inside it is breathtakingly beautiful. It is decorated with colourful wall frescoes that have survived for centuries and is well worthy of its place on UNESCO's World Heritage list. F7

12 PEDOULÁS ★

The mountain village can boast two special attractions: it's a centre of cherry cultivation and probably has the highest density of churches on Cyprus. Pedoulás's divine protection comes from ten churches – the most appealing of which is the small barn-roofed church *Ágios Michaíl (free*

admission, donations accepted) with wall frescoes that date back over 500 years. Apart from this you can find handmade souvenirs in one of the many small shops on the main street (preserved fruits, wood carvings) and from the terrace of the *Two Flowers Hotel*, you can admire the main church in the valley and the houses that cling to the slopes like swallows' nests. *E7*

13 KALOPANAGIÓTIS

Climbing up and down the steep, sloping streets is a thing of the past. The village has funded a funicular which transports visitors to the monastery down in the valley and back. There is a fabulous panoramic view across the countryside to the reservoir. The village is also well known for its sulphurous springs and is popular with amateur photographers who find plenty of inspiration in the idyllic rural surroundings here. In the Soujoúkos Factory on the outskirts of the village, the sweet Cypriot speciality is made all year round. Strings of almonds or walnuts are immersed in grape syrup and the resulting "snakes" are left to dry on the terrace of the factory – it's so photogenic, you'll find it hard to resist!

The region's historical attraction is the monastery of *Ágios Giánnis Lampadistís (daily 9am–1pm and 4–6pm; winter 3–5pm | free admission)*. It houses valuable frescos mainly dating from the 13th and 15th centuries. Old agricultural equipment such as an oil and wine press have been carefully installed in the former monastery cells. Even those who are not keen on Christian icons will be interested in the monastery's *Museum (Mon–Sat 9.30am–6pm, low and late season 9.30am–5pm; winter 10am–3.30pm | admission 1 euro)*. In the exhibition, the pictures are displayed as though they have a heavenly radiance. It's a question of quality, not quantity. *E7*

14 KÝKKO MONASTERY ★

A rainmaker lives high up on this mountain. At least, that's what the legend says – the icon of the Virgin Mary in Kýkko Monastery supposedly has a positive influence on the weather. It's a useful skill to conjure up rains in an arid landscape. And as a result, it is not surprising that Kýkko accrued wealth in the form of generous sacrificial offerings. The gold is proudly displayed on the icons, chandeliers and porcelain mosaics in the arcades. The portrait of Panagía (Mary) is hidden behind gold and silver. At an altitude of 1,200m, Kýkko is an ideal spot for a trip into the mountains.

The floors of the *Museum* are decorated with colourful granite and marble; the ceilings are decorated with walnut and gold leaf. *Daily 10am–6pm; winter 10am–4pm | admission 5 euros*

Surrounding the monastery are numerous booths (let out by the monastery) that sell souvenirs.

INSIDER TIP
Monks' tipple

You can take home the unusual red Zivania, which is distilled by the monks here – its colour is derived from the cinnamon and other spices used as botanicals, and it tastes milder than the clear original. You can, of course, also buy it from the shops around the monastery, almost at source. From the restaurant here, there is a fabulous view over the mountainous countryside. D7

PIT-STOP BARBECUES

PICNIC SPOTS

There are 40 picnic spots in southern Cyprus's forests and woods. They are all very well equipped with tables, benches, fire pits, toilets and playgrounds. Some have space for up to 1,600 people, some for 50. At the weekend, Cypriots come up into the mountains bringing everything but the kitchen sink with them for *souvla* barbecues. Wine and games are all part of the fun so don't be surprised to see lots of people passed out as the day wears on! Unfortunately, the leaflet "Picnic and Camping Sites in the State Forests of Cyprus" has gone out of print, but you can access it online at short.travel/zyp8.

WINE ROUTES 4–6

Four of Cyprus's seven wine routes pass through the Tróodos mountains above Limassol. Route no. 4 takes you to the Krasochória, where the most traditional wine-producing villages (Ómodos, Arsos, Maliá, Koiláni and Vouní) are grouped together. The villages which produces the oldest wine type in the world are to be found in the Commandaria region (route no. 5) which centres on the villages of Zoopigí and Kaló Chorió. The Pitsiliá route (no. 6) winds its way through the villages of Agrós, Kyperoúnta (try the white wine "Petritis" made using the Xinistreri grape *(photiadesgroup.com/kyperounda)* and Peléndri.

EATING & DRINKING

The most fantastic restaurants can be discovered in the smallest villages of the Tróodos mountains. The network of traditional tavernas is expanding thanks to the growth of agrotourism.

ARIADNI

35km / 45 mins from Limassol by car

She can certainly cook! This remote taverna only serves home-made delicacies made by Ms Ariadni herself. Her potatoes roasted in wine and coriander are a dream. *Wed–Mon lunch noon–4pm, dinner from 6pm | Vása Kilaniou, approx. 1km outside the village | tel. 25 94 40 64 | € | E9*

MYLOS (MILL)

55km / 70 mins from Nicosia by car

The restaurant on the upper floor of the architecturally interesting *Mill Hotel* is among the best in Cyprus. Particularly delicious is the salmon trout with an olive oil/lemon-garlic sauce. *Daily from noon | reservation recommended | Kakopetriá | tel. 22 92 25 36 | millhotelcyprus.com | €€ | F7*

ORÉA ELLAS

30km / 40 mins from Limassol by car

When modernity and tradition meet, you can get sensational results and this is a perfect example. The restaurant is housed in a traditional farmhouse, but the food is the result of a creative partnership between an actor and a director. Both cook extremely well and they know how to host a fun evening too. *Fri 7–10pm, Sat 1–6.30pm and 7–10pm, Sun 1–5pm | Vouní | tel. 25 94 43 28 | IG: Horea Ellas – Vouni | €€ | E9*

SKYLIGHT

35km / 45 mins from Limassol by car

Elegance and luxury in the heart of the mountains. The food and wines are excellent. The desserts are simply sensational. Then there is the terrace with a pool – it's simply unbeatable! *Daily 9am–11pm | 524 Archbishop Makarios | Páno Plátres | tel. 25 42 22 44 | skylight.com.cy | €€€ | E8*

Follow a wine route through Tróodos

SYMPÓSIO

37km / 45 mins from Limassol by car

Food aplenty! The generous mezé made from the freshest ingredients (salad from the garden) attracts gourmet diners. *Tue–Thu noon–3pm, Fri/Sat noon–11pm, Sun noon–6pm | Pelendri, turn off at the crossroads of highways 806 and 801 | tel. 99 40 43 48 | symposiocyprus.com | €€ | F8*

SPORT & ACTIVITIES

ADVENTURE MOUNTAIN PARK

40km / 50 mins from Limassol by car

The Adventure Mountain Park in Kyperoúnta is popular for outdoor action: laser tag, rock climbing, archery, abseiling. If the adrenalin levels get too high, take a break in the herb garden or restaurant. They have a campsite too. *Tue–Sun 9am–8pm; winter 8am–6pm | climbing 17 euros/hr, laser tag 7 euros/20 mins | adventuremountainpark.com | F8*

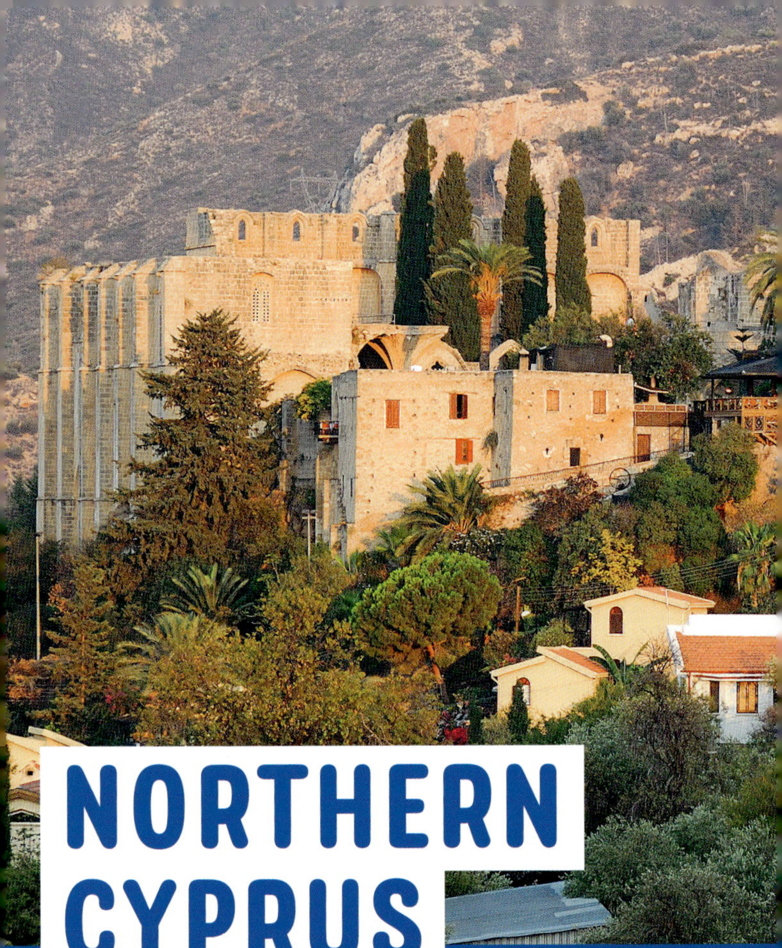

NORTHERN CYPRUS

UNDIVIDED BEAUTY

Once you show your passport at the checkpoint, you head into a state that is not recognised by 192 out of 193 member states of the United Nations: the Turkish Republic of Northern Cyprus. Nevertheless, don't be fooled into thinking the northern part of the island is defined by chaos and anarchy.

This "illegal" country has criminally beautiful beaches and plenty of charm. Its population of around 300,000 people is similar to the

The mountain village of Bellapaís has a ruined Gothic abbey

average London borough, and the way of life here is, in many ways, hardly distinguishable from that in the south of the island.

Most travellers are attracted by the amazing landscape – from the "Five Finger" mountain to the sparsely populated Karpas peninsula and the gently rolling foothills of the Tróodos mountains, which slip gently into the sea at Morfou Bay. Apart from north Nicosia, the only significant towns are Kerýneia and Famagusta.

NORTHERN CYPRUS

Mesógeios Thálassa
(Mediterranean Sea)
75km, 1½ hrs
20km, 40 mins
Kerýneia Castle
Kerýneia
p. 112
8 Alagadi (Alakati) Turtle Beach
1 Bellapaís (Beylerbeyi)
Bellapaís Abbey
Escape Beach Club
Green Heights 3
St Hilárion 2
Blue Villa (Mavi Köşk)
3
Akdeniz Beach
5 Akdeniz (Agía Eiríni)
4 Historic Olive Grove
7 Soli
65km, 1 hr 20 mins
6 Vouní
Lefke
Κοκκινοτριμιθιά
Kokkinotrimithia
A9
Λευκωσία
Lefkoşa
Nicosia
Aslanköy
Στρόβολος
Strovolos
Akdoğan
Evrychou
Pera
Dali
Athienou/Kiracıköy
A2
Αραδίππου
Aradhippou
CYPRUS
ΚΥΠΡΟΣ - KIBRIS
Tróodos
Λάρνακα
Larnaca
A5
Eptagoneia
Kofinou
Parekklisia
A1
Επισκοπή
Episkopi
A6
Λεμεσός
Limassol
British Sovereign Base Areas
10 km
6.21 mi

Apóstolos Andréas Monastery
20
Ágios Philon ★ 18
Golden Beach 19
17 Dipkarpaz (Rizokárpaso)
16 Ágios Thýrsos
Büyükkonuk (Kómi Kepir) ★
14
15 Kumyali (Kóma Tou Gialoú)
Minia Kibris 10
Kantára 13
9 İncirli Cave ★
İskele
Trikomo
Geçitkale
95km, 2 hrs
12 Melandra House
11 Sálamis ★
Dörtyol
Famagusta
p. 118
Δερύνεια
Deryneia
Παραλίμνι
Paralimni
British Sovereign
Base Areas
A3
Αγία Νάπα
Ayia Napa
Ξυλοφάγου
Xylofagou

MARCO POLO HIGHLIGHTS

★ **KERÝNEIA CASTLE**
Scary dungeon and a boat that is as old as Archimedes ➤ p. 112

★ **BELLAPAÍS ABBEY**
Music now plays where monks once dined ➤ p. 115

★ **ALAGADI (ALAKATI) TURTLE BEACH**
Watch how sea turtles live ➤ p. 117

★ **İNCIRLI CAVE**
The only accessible land cave on the whole island ➤ p. 117

★ **SÁLAMIS**
An ancient Roman spa, complete with pillars and a public latrine ➤ p. 121

★ **BÜYÜKKONUK (KÓMI KEPIR)**
A hands-on eco-holiday: baking bread, weaving baskets and making cheese ➤ p. 122

★ **ÁGIOS PHILON**
Romantic sunsets with ruins, palm trees and delicious food ➤ p. 122

KERÝNEIA/ GIRNE

(📖 J4) **Once thought of as the "pearl of the Mediterranean", Kerýneia has long since cast off much of its small-town atmosphere but its charm has remained. To get yourselves in the holiday spirit, take a walk along the harbour and stop for a drink somewhere with a view over the bustle of boats big and small.**

The thick walls of the castle, which are the town's most famous landmark, are right next to the promenade. There are no suburbs; where the small town (27,000 inhabitants) stops, the rugged Pendedaktylos mountains begin. The proximity of the rural hinterlands makes Kerýneia the perfect base for a holiday spent among castles, turtles, beaches, caves and mountains.

SIGHTSEEING

KERÝNEIA CASTLE ★

Cameras at the ready! From these fortifications, you have the most fabulous views of the harbour and mountains. The city's emblem was used for centuries as a fortification and dungeon. And the chaotic network of dark passageways, dungeons and vaults is still enough to send a shiver down your spine. The castle offers free tours from the ticket hut so long as you have a group of four to six people. In the castle courtyard, the *Shipwreck Museum* and café are ideal. *April–Oct*

INSIDER TIP
Group tours if there is a group ...

CAFE CHIMERA

Kerýneia's relaxed harbour promenade is lined with cafés and restaurants *daily 8am–7pm; Nov–March daily 8am–3.30pm | admission 152 TL | ⏲ 1 hr*

SHIPWRECK MUSEUM

These planks are genuine (don't try and walk them!) and date from the time when Archimedes invented the pulley. The trading ship, around which the museum is based, sank 2,300 years ago off the coast of Kerýneia. Its wreck and some of the cargo were so well preserved that they gave researchers a whole new perspective on trading routes in the Mediterranean and ancient shipbuilding. The wine amphoras and almonds, which were on board, are displayed in the museum. *April–Oct daily 8am–7pm; Nov–March daily 8am–3.30pm | admission included in the ticket to the castle | ⏲ 1 hr*

EFES

PORT OF KERÝNEIA

The small port in Kerýneia has a special atmosphere. It's a heady mixture of the romanticism of fishing boats, a place to stroll on a Sunday afternoon and the buzz of tourism. Where today tourist boats drop anchor and their passengers enjoy sipping a beer was once a mooring for the ships of the Byzantines and Venetians. Right in the entrance to the harbour you can make out a ruined tower from which, in medieval times, a chain could be pulled across to what is today the Customs House, as a form of protection against unwanted guests. On the pier, fishermen spend their days hoping for the next big catch; you can join them with a book on one of the benches or take a stroll up to the romantic lighthouse.

CAROB STORE/CYPRUS HOUSE

This little museum is housed in one of the old carob stores in the port. Its collection comprises historic agricultural machinery downstairs, while upstairs there is a replica of a 18th-century Cypriot house. There is also a documentary to watch with footage from Cyprus in the 1930s. *Mon–Fri 8am–3.30pm | admission 95 TL | ⏲ 30 mins*

EATING & DRINKING

If you've only got one day in Kerýneia, the most atmospheric places for food with a view can be found at the harbour, though there are numerous taverns in the town and in the neighbouring bays.

O PSARÁS ÁPO TO ZYGÍ (CANLI BALIK)

A Turkish Cypriot, who before 1974 used to be a fisherman in the southern Cypriot town of Zygí, today runs the fish restaurant at the harbour. So you won't be surprised to learn that its Greek name translates as "The fisherman from Zygí". *Daily 10am–midnight | harbour promenade | €€*

SIMIT DÜNYASI

Forget the word "diet" when you enter this cake shop. This is the perfect spot in Kerýneia to indulge your appetite for gourmet sweet treats. The best *simits* (sesame rings) in town are to be found here and the best news of all? They are a traditional breakfast snack but you can have them all day. *Daily 8am–11pm | Kordonboyu promenade park/corner of Atatürk Cd*

INSIDER TIP
Rings of joy

SPORT & ACTIVITIES

Boat trips with stops for swimming or fishing are offered in the harbour by, for example, *Aphrodite Boat Tours (kyreniaboattrips.com)*. The best conditions for kitesurfing are in Morfou Bay. Paragliding and deep-sea fishing trips can be booked at *Highline Air Tours'* office in the port *(highline paragliding.com)*. *Amphora Diving Center (amphoradiving.com)* is a good diving school. The most beautiful hike on the ridge of the Kerýneia Mountains starts from *Besparmak Bufavento Restaurant* on the pass.

BEACHES

There are no beaches in Kerýneia, only spots from which you can access the sea from the rocky coast. To swim, take your hire car, the bus or a taxi to neighbouring bays: *Acapulco Beach* (10km east), *Lara Beach* (12km east) or *Deniz Kizi Beach* (8km west). All of the above are public beaches. There are also places where you can pay admission (usually around 375 TL) and get the full (in theory less crowded) beach experience; one good option is the *Escape Beach Club* (6km west).

NIGHTLIFE

There are going out and clubbing options both in the town, for example *Groggy Lounge (midnight–3am | Iskenderun Cd | FB: Groggy Lounge)*, and on the beaches, where *Club Locca* on Escape Beach is currently the most popular place *(Fri/Sat from 10pm | FB: Escape Beach)*. If you want to live the high life, there are 13 casinos offering gambling, shows and other entertainment.

AROUND KERÝNEIA/ GIRNE

1 BELLAPAÍS (BEYLERBEYI)

6km / 15 mins from Kerýneia by car

This pretty mountain village south of Kerýneia can boast some of the most

TELEPHONE

A mulberry tree provides a shady spot for a snack near Bellapaís Abbey

romantic ruins in the country. The magnificent ★ *Gothic abbey* dates from the 14th century *(summer daily 9am–8pm; winter daily 9am–4.45pm | admission 114 TL | ⏲ 30 mins)*. The refectory – now the concert hall – has the best acoustics on Cyprus (Classical Music Festival in May/June).

The abbey at night is beautifully lit and is well worth sticking around for, especially if you combine it with dinner at the hotel *Bellapaís Gardens' restaurant (daily from 7pm | reserve ahead | tel. 0392 8 15 60 66 | bellapaisgardens.com)*. Their food is excellent and sustainably sourced and, sitting by their pool, you won't regret staying for the evening.

Bellapaís is also where Cyprus's most famous tree once stood. In his book *Bitter Lemons* Lawrence Durrell describes the "tree of idleness", whose pleasant shade it is almost impossible to leave. The mulberry tree has long since succumbed to eternal idleness but all the cafés by the abbey still claim to be able to enchant you into spending a whole day there. *🕮 J4*

2 ST HILÁRION

9km / 15 mins from Kerýneia by car

Dreeaaamy! The ruin is more like a palace than a castle, since it was converted in the 13th century into a summer royal residence. And, of course, they bagged themselves the best sea views around. Those who prefer not to go up to the main castle can stay below in the *café (the same opening hours as for the castle)*. From here, the view is almost as beautiful. *Daily 9am–5pm | admission 152 TL | 1.5 hrs | H4*

3 BLUE VILLA (MAVI KÖŞK)

30km / 40 mins from Kerýneia by car

The Blue Villa (Mavi Köşk) is an extremely bizarre attraction. It is decorated in 1960s style with extravagant furnishings and artworks. The eccentric owner, Byron Pavlides, supposedly held wild parties here. According to rumours, the building near Çamlıbel (Mýrtou) has secret corridors that were used as a hiding place for smuggled goods. This "museum" with its beautifully designed garden and wonderful view is on a Turkish military base and is only accessible for visitors with a passport or ID card. *Tue–Sun 10am–4pm | admission free | Myrtou (Çamlıbel) | 1 hr | G4*

4 HISTORIC OLIVE GROVE

41km / 55 mins from Kerýneia by car

Some of the olive trees in this valley are around 800 years old. Their gnarled trunks make for great, atmospheric photos. *Freely accessible | Kapoúti (Kalkanlı) | 1 hr | F5*

5 AKDENIZ (AGÍA EIRÍNI)

40km / 50 mins from Kerýneia by car

The west coast of Northern Cyprus is still unspoilt by tourism. On *Akdeniz Beach*, 40km from Kerýneia, there is only one restaurant, *Caretta Beach (FB: Akdeniz Caretta Beach & Restaurant | €)*. It doubles up as a travel agent for excellent ecotourism day trips. Picnics, horse and cart rides, and visits to shepherds and farmers in the mountains all come as part of the deal. *E5*

6 VOUNÍ

65km / 80 mins from Kerýneia by car

What a view! The ruins of a palace perched on the flat summit of a 255m hill. The palace was once spread over three floors and contained 140 rooms alongside a thermal bath area. Walking through the ruins and looking out over the bay of Mórfou, you will find it hard not to hand it to the palace's original builders: they could hardly have picked a better place to live. *April–Oct daily 8am–6pm; Nov–March daily 8am–3.30pm | Admission 95 TL | 30 mins | E6*

INSIDER TIP Fish pitstop

Amazingly there is only one informal fish restaurant in Northern Cyprus. *Merhaba Balik Evi (Fri–Wed noon–midnight | Karavostasi (Gemikonaği) | FB: Merhaba Balik Evi | €)* is on the way to Vouní and is well worth a stop. With tables directly on the beach, there are worse places to watch the sun go down!

7 SOLI

70km / 1 hr from Kerýneia by car

The ruins of this Iron Age city kingdom are best known for the magical swan mosaic found in an early Christian basilica. But there are also temple remains and a Roman amphitheatre, from whose terraces you can enjoy a magnificent view of the coastal landscape. *Daily 9am–6pm, winter until 4pm | admission 112 TL | Gemikonaği (Lefke) | 1.5 hrs | E6*

8 ALAGADI (ALAKATI) TURTLE BEACH ★

16.5km / 30 mins from Kerýneia by car

The most thrilling natural spectacle on Cyprus! Join animal welfare campaigners from the *Turtle Conservation Station* as they take part in a night watch to observe female turtles laying their eggs on the beach. A few weeks later you can see how the baby turtles leave their nests and crawl into the water. The information point is open every day from May to September 9am–8.30pm and is located 500m from the main beach. Registration is essential for both tours. This is a highly popular thing to do on Cyprus and places are limited, so book online to avoid disappointment. *Nightwatch suggested donation 375 TL | cyprusturles.org | Night-watch 3 hrs, hatching 2 hrs | K4*

INSIDER TIP **Booking advised**

9 İNCIRLI CAVE ★

48km / 1 hr from Kerýneia by car

Crawl into the underbelly of Cyprus! Well, not exactly crawl, as İncirli Cave near *Platáni (Çınarlı)* is big enough to stand up in. It is even illuminated so that the glittering gypsum crystal is displayed to full effect. At a length of 70m, this is the biggest cave on the island. It's named after the fig tree (Turkish: *İncir*) that almost conceals the entrance and supposedly has healing powers. The path to the cave, which is just outside the village, is signposted. *Thu–Tue 8am–3pm | admission 114 TL | Platani (Çınarlı) | M4*

10 MINIA KIBRIS

43km / 50 mins from Kerýneia by car

Bird's eye view! Northern Cyprus's main sights are all gathered here ... in miniature. From castles to mosques and churches, there is no better place to get an overview of what the northern part of the island has to offer. *Daily 8am–5pm | admission 95 TL | Akanthoú (Tatlisu) | 30 mins | M4*

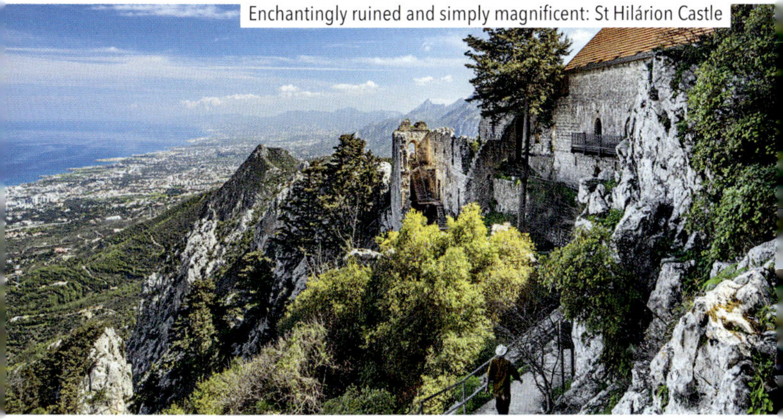

Enchantingly ruined and simply magnificent: St Hilárion Castle

FAMAGUSTA

(📖 N6) **Over 650 years ago Famagusta was the easternmost port in the western world and, as a result, it became a hub for all kinds of luxury products – from spices to silk and carpets. Today, the ruins of churches and palaces in the old town are the only reminders of the town's former wealth. Nowadays, Famagusta (pop. 42,000) wears the scars of modern development and its precarious political position, which has turned it into an odd mix of forgotten port and endless sandy beach, which is partly fenced off and lined with hotel ruins. The true treasure of this region is hidden just outside the city: the Karpas peninsula.**

SIGHTSEEING

LALA MUSTAFA PASHA MOSQUE

In Famagusta's heyday, the Frankish kingdom on Cyprus donated a second cathedral. It took 28 years to complete and was consecrated in 1326 at the same time as Sophia Cathedral in Nicosia. Its magnificent western façade is reminiscent of a French Gothic cathedral. Only the addition of a minaret reveals that the church was turned into a mosque in 1571. *Freely accessible | 🕒 30 mins*

LAND GATE & CITY WALLS

From the city walls you get a fabulous view of Famagusta (once a practical defence mechanism, today a handy way to get your bearings) The walls are 7m thick and up to 18m high. Built in the 16th century, they were at the forefront of military technology. There are 15 bastions along their 3km. Ultimately, the effort was to no avail, as the Ottoman conquerors simply starved the occupants of the fortress during the occupation. The Turkish name for the Land Gate is *Akkule* or "White Tower", as it was here that the Venetians raised their first white flag in 1571 as a sign of their surrender. The narrow streets of the old town make it a nightmare best avoided by cars. The best way to avoid the difficulty of parking in the city's old town is to drive around the edge to the Sea Gate. Once inside, you will find plenty of parking opposite the Othello Tower.

INSIDER TIP
Stress-free parking

OTHELLO TOWER

Death and murder in the harbour! That's how Shakespeare imagined life in Famagusta. In his play, the Moorish prince and general in the Venetian army, Othello, strangles his wife in a jealous rage and then stabs himself. It is unknown whether or not the Bard had the citadel in the harbour at Famagusta in mind when he wrote the tragedy. Whatever the case, the tragedy is set in this town and the castle is known as "Othello Tower". *Daily 8am–7pm, winter until 3.30pm | admission 114 TL | 🕒 30 mins*

BANDABULIYA

The former market hall, Bandabuliya, has become a shopping district. After

The Lala Mustafa Mosque was founded in 1326 as a Gothic cathedral

butchers and grocers gave up their stores here, souvenir shops and cafés moved in. Inside it has become something of a meeting place for all kinds of local groups and it can be hard to find a seat, but many attractive spots have developed outside. *Opposite Lala Mustafa Mosque | ⏲ 30 mins (incl. a cup of coffee)*

VARÓSHA

Once upon a time, this was the buzziest place on Cyprus. Until 1974, Varósha was the island's top tourist destination. Then the Turkish army arrived and claimed the territory. Holidaymakers and residents immediately cleared out and left everything behind. All that remained were hotel ruins, abandoned houses and an untouched sandy beach. Since 2020, the former Turkish military site has been opened to the public in sections. Despite the protests of the displaced owners, Varósha is to be rebuilt as a holiday destination.

EATING & DRINKING

D & B

The most modern restaurant in the Old Town. Pizzas, pasta, salads, steaks, kebabs. *Daily from 10am | Namık Kemal Meydanı 14 | €€*

DE MOLAY

This hip bar has taken up residence in the historic walls of an old Crusader church. Where the Templars and Knights of St John had their headquarters in the 13th century, craft beer and cocktails are now served. *Mon–Thu 11.30am–2am, Fri/Sat until 2.30am | Kışla Yolu Sokak | €€*

PETEK PASTANESI

Prepare to be seduced. The best patisserie in the Old Town for Turkish treats and light snacks. *Daily 7am–midnight | Yesil Deniz Sok. 1 | €€*

TAŞKIN'IN YERI

With this restaurant just a few metres from the harbour's quay, you won't find fresher fish anywhere on the island. It's so close to the action of the port that it is not the easiest place to find – keep your eyes peeled just after entering the port area. *Daily 11am–12.30am | tel. 0533 852 53 69 | Liman Içi | €€*

INSIDER TIP
The only restaurant in the port

SPORT & ACTIVITIES

Thanks to a combination of stunning landscape and virtually empty roads (which wind beautifully through the hills), Famagusta is a good place to get on a bike and explore. *Velespeed (74 TL/hr | en.velespeed.net)*, for example, operates bike-sharing stations. The *Dive Hub* diving school *(from 65 euros | Bogaz | dive-hub.com)* offers a wide range of diving courses off the coast of Famagusta, including Bubblemaker courses for children aged eight and over, night diving, deep diving and underwater photography.

BEACHES

The beach at Palm Beach Hotel does not charge for access. However, for a good swim you're better off heading out to the long – and also free – sandy beach in front of the excavations of Sálamis, where you can combine some historical exploration with a refreshing dip.

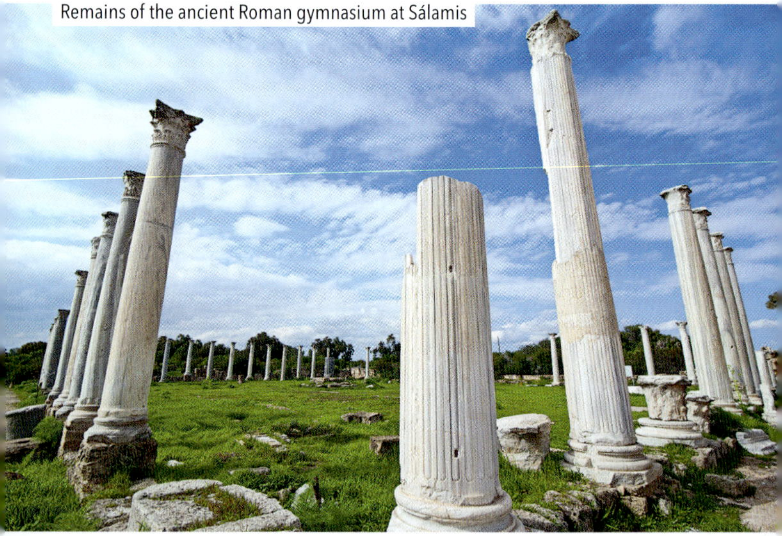

Remains of the ancient Roman gymnasium at Sálamis

NIGHTLIFE

The old town is fairly dead at nighttime. All the action is in the students' quarter around the university *(Ismet Inöni Bulvar)*. Another hip location is the *Lions Garden (weekends from 10pm | street after Sálamis | FB: Lions Garden Club)*, which is a mixture of disco, club and concert hall behind a showy façade.

AROUND FAMAGUSTA

11 SÁLAMIS ★

9km / 15 mins from Famagusta by car

Where did people do business in ancient times? On the loo! The shared facilities that allowed this to happen are on display at the burial site in Sálamis. Water rushed through a stone channel beneath the 44-seat latrine. The toilet belonged to a gymnasium complex that is well preserved. The area lined with columns was a training ground for physical education for men. Alongside it was a swimming pool and thermal baths.

You get the best sense of the spread of this ancient site from the upper rows of the Roman amphitheatre, which had a seating capacity for 15,000 spectators. Today, it is a concert venue whose atmosphere is very special indeed. *May–Sept daily 9am–7pm; Oct–April daily 9am–3.30pm | admission to excavations 114 TL | 1.5 hrs | N5*

12 MELANDRA HOUSE

13km / 20 mins from Famagusta by car

A true replica of the original family home, which the owner has lovingly decorated with furniture and accessories collected and saved over 30 years. Tools, household items and furniture from the pre-war period are displayed inside the house and around the lovely green courtyard.

INSIDER TIP The right way to start your day

The best Cypriot breakfast on the island is served up here at the weekend with fresh fruit, home-made bread and grilled halloumi. Make sure you try the toast dunked in carob syrup! *Daily 9am–5pm | main road in the direction of Karpas | tel. 0533 8 61 97 04 | FB: Melandra House | € | N5*

13 KANTÁRA

35km / 50 mins from Famagusta by car

From up here you can see the north and south coasts at the same time! The ruins of a Crusader castle sit majestically at 630m on a rock and guarantee an incredible view of the surrounding countryside.

INSIDER TIP Be there first or last thing!

The views are at their best at sunrise and sunset. And, what's more, nobody mans the admission kiosk at these times and the entrance is never locked. *May–Sept daily 8am–5pm; Oct–April daily 8am–3.30pm | admission 95 TL | 1.5 hrs (including climb) | N4*

14 BÜYÜKKONUK (KÓMI KEPIR)

★ *40km / 50 mins from Famagusta by car*

This is where ecotourism on Northern Cyprus was practically invented. The village is streets ahead of other local communities, with rustic B&Bs, organic markets and activities for tourists. The local women's group offers courses in traditional crafts from soap-making to weaving and brush-making. There are eco festivals in May and October to which all visitors are invented. *eco tourismcyprus.com* | *O3*

15 KUMYALI (KÓMA TOU GIALOÚ)

45km / 50 mins from Famagusta by car

You can spend a while in this village which has a beach and fishing marina, as well as secret spots to discover nearby – ideal hiding places for geocaching! There is an underground Phoenician tomb site, a Byzantine olive mill and an enchanting lagoon that ends in the white dunes of a beach. *P3*

16 ÁGIOS THÝRSOS

60km / 75 mins from Famagusta by car

If you plan to start a family, pay close attention: beneath *Ágios Thýrsos* church directly by the sea is a small chapel with a rock crevice, where a magical spring flows. According to legend, the holy water from here is said to fulfil women's desire for children. The chapel is filled with pictures of saints and wishes written on small pieces of paper. Opposite the church, a path leads inland to a mysterious discovery: between the rocks and bushes are two roughly 3m-high stone statues (with no signs) which look as if they could be Egyptian. Or perhaps they are from the Bronze Age. Archaeologists don't seem to be much interested in them. *2 hrs (inc. walk to the statues)* | *Q2*

INSIDER TIP
Do a bit of Indiana Jones-ing

17 DIPKARPAZ (RIZOKÁRPASO)

80km / 1 hr 40 mins from Famagusta by car

This is the last settlement before the splendid isolation of the Karpas peninsula. You can spend a day on one of the stunning beaches near the village, then find a place to stay and avoid the long drive back to civilisation after a hard day's relaxation. This is where you should stock up on snacks and drinks for your day at the beach. Apart from that, the village does not offer much in terms of excitement. If you are up for trying a local snack, the best *lahmacun*, or Middle Eastern pizza, is available from *Dostlar* (*daily 11am–11pm | on the road out towards the Apóstolos Andréas monastery | €*). Give it a try! You can either eat it warm straight away or save it for the beach/drive home. *Q–R2*

INSIDER TIP
The best food in the village

18 ÁGIOS PHILON ★

85km / 1 hr 45 mins from Famagusta by car

Are you looking for the perfect place to watch a sunset? You won't find much better than the *Oasis* restaurant on the north coast of the Karpas peninsula

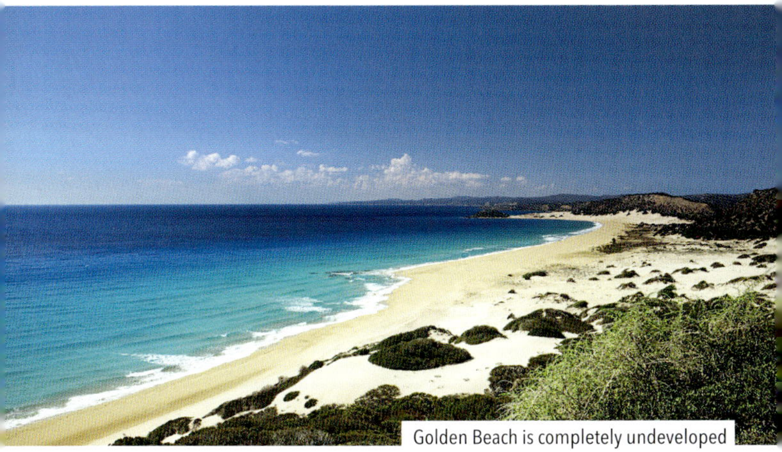

Golden Beach is completely undeveloped

(tel. 0542 8 56 50 82 | oasis hotelkarpas.com | €). This location offers palm trees, the ruined *Ágios Philon* church and an unspoiled view of the sea. You look out over a sandy beach along the crescent-shaped bay, which is also a breeding site for turtles. *Q1*

19 GOLDEN BEACH

95km / 1 hr 45 mins from Famagusta by car

Tucked away behind sand dunes bordering on agricultural fields, *Golden Beach* stretches for 3km up the coast to the *Apóstolos Andréas Monastery*. Nature is left to its own devices here and the only things interrupting your view will be sun, sand and sea … oh, and an occasional human, but even in summer not many bother to come out here. All the better for you! Up until now, a ban on building has ensured that there are no hotels. Water sports are also prohibited. If you settle in here for a day of sunshine you are here to enjoy nature. *R–S1*

20 APÓSTOLOS ANDRÉAS MONASTERY

95km / 1 hr 45 mins from Famagusta by car

Do you believe in miracles? Then you should definitely try a few drops from the spring at the foot of the monastery. The water is meant to have healing properties for almost everything. That's thanks to St Andrew. On one of his voyages in the first century, the drinking water on his ship had run out. The Apostle ordered the crew to beat their swords against a rock, and – lo and behold – a well began to gush water. During a later trip, the ship's captain left an icon depicting the apostle at this site, which became the foundation of the monastery. *Freely accessible |*

From here, you can follow a footpath along the coast for 5km to the very tip of the island of Cyprus, at Cape Apóstolos Andréas. *S1*

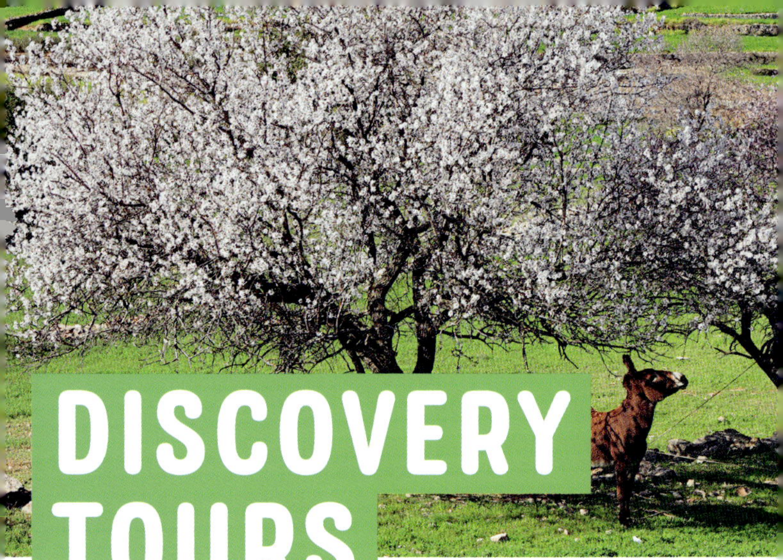

DISCOVERY TOURS

Do you want to get under the skin of the island? Then our discovery tours provide the perfect guide – they include advice on which sights to visit, tips on where to stop for that perfect holiday snap, a choice of the best places to eat and drink and suggestions for fun activities.

1 MOUNT ÓLYMPOS – ATALANTA TRAIL

- Views across the island in all directions
- A nature trail with added adventure at an old mine
- Cool mountain air and plenty of shade – the perfect summer walk

Tróodos

Tróodos

Half day (4.5 hrs total walking time)

Distance: 15km

Difficulty: very easy

Information: Well-marked path. Bring a picnic and a torch to explore the old mine shaft.

1
2
3

The Tróodos mountains are particularly peaceful in springtime

DIVE INTO THE PEACEFUL LANDSCAPE AND BREATHE IN NATURE'S PERFUME

What makes the Atalanta Trail so special is that the 1m- to 3m-wide path has plenty of shade. Park up in ❶ Tróodos ➤ p. 102 where the trail begins. *Leave the crowded village square at the uppermost fork in the road* and within seconds you will find yourself surrounded by deafening and refreshing silence. It is after all no accident that the path is named Atalanta after a woodland nymph from Greek mythology. On a clear day, you'll be able to make out the Akrotíri peninsula. In spring, the ❷ rock roses along the path are in full bloom. In summer, the plant's leaves excrete a resin, which gives off an enchanting smell and is commonly used in chypre perfumes.

❶ **Tróodos**
2km 35 mins

❷ **rock roses**
500m 7 mins

PICNIC UNDER ANCIENT JUNIPERS

Oaks are not just a feature of cold and damp climates. On the mountain here, you will see lots of ❸ holm oaks , which can be identified by their acorns and shiny leaves. Much rarer, though, are the so-called ❹ strawberry trees that grow in this area. The name is misleading and the fruits don't (as far as we know) go well with cream. But they are easily recognisable all

❸ **holm oaks**
1.2km 16 mins

❹ **strawberry trees**
1.5km 30 mins

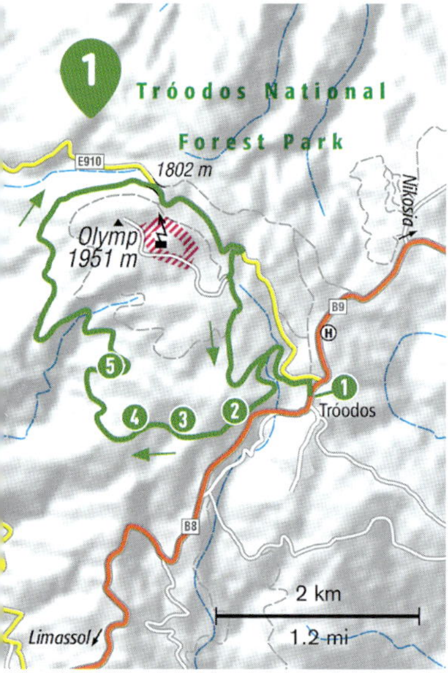
1
Tróodos National Forest Park
E910
1802 m
Olymp
1951 m
Nikosia
B9
Tróodos
B8
2 km
1.2 mi
Limassol

year round thanks to their very smooth red trunks making them easy to spot. Smooth surfaces like this are rare in nature and you may find the temptation to run your hand along them irresistible. *About a third of the way into the hike,* you will come across an area where ancient juniper trees provide much-needed shade. Some of the trees are 500–700 years old and have offered generations of walkers a cool spot to settle down with a picnic. There is even a small spring where you can top up your water bottle.

TAKE A LOOK INTO THE EARTH'S BELLY

5 abandoned mine

9.5km 2 hrs 45 mins

This is where it gets interesting! *After about 5km you will pass the entrance to* **5 an abandoned mine** in which chromium ore was mined until 1982. Turn on your torch and venture a few yards into the shaft at your own risk.

Trees provide welcome shade for walkers on this route

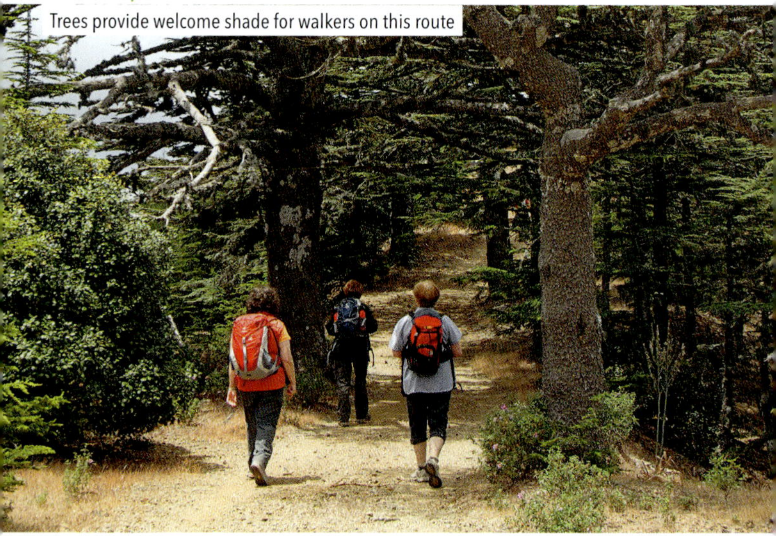

THE FINAL PUSH!

After almost 10km the trail reaches the tarmac road leading from Tróodos up to Mount Ólympos. The peak itself is located in a restricted military area, so it does not pay to take a detour to the top. *Instead, keep to the right and follow signs back to* ① Tróodos The best spot for some well-earned refreshment is the terrace of the Tróodos Hotel *(troodoshotel.com).*

① Tróodos

② WALKING NEAR AGÍA NÁPA

- Wonder at the spectacular sea caves
- Walk on a natural stone arch with the sea beneath you
- Stop to swim and snorkel whenever you want

Cape Gréko bus stop

Kónnos Beach bus stop

Half day (2hrs total walking time)

Distance: 7km

Difficulty: Easy

Information: In the summer, make sure you set off by 8am, otherwise you will be walking in the heat of the day. Bring a sunhat and swimming stuff! In summer, buses nos. 101 and 102 run every 20–30 minutes from Agía Nápa to Paralímni (6.15am–midnight); in winter they are less frequent. (Timetable: *osea.com.cy*).

WAVE YOUR TROUBLES GOODBYE

From the ① Cape Gréko bus stop *on the main road, a narrow tarmac road leads away from the villages into the* Cape Gréko National Park. In spring, this landscape erupts into colour as the trees begin to blossom, and in the summer it plays host to a marvellously Mediterranean soundscape as the buzz of insects interacts with the pitter-patter of geckos running across rocks, while the sea gently laps the coast below. Any stress you're feeling will disappear as fast as the geckos. To get

① Cape Gréko bus stop

1.9km 30 mins

Cyclops Cave
E306
Kávo Gkréko National Forest Park
Kónnos Bay
Agíi Anárgyri
Kamára tou Koráka
Sea Caves
Viewpoint Cavos
93 m
Kávo Gkréko
N
2 km
1.2 mi

to the walk's first major highlight *walk about 600m along the road and then, at the sign, take the path across the fields for a 600m-long path* until you get to the spectacular ❷ sea caves. The bay here is about 1km long and its cliffs have formed into a series of perfectly round caves which stretch all the way across its length.

INSIDER TIP
Taking the grot out of grottoes

THROUGH THE GATE TO THE WORLD BEYOND

Return to the small road, which you are going to follow until you reach Cape Gréko National Park's Environmetal Centre. *About 500m further on,* you will find yourself at a portal to the big, wide world. Or at least that is how it seems when the light perfectly glints off the azure sea through the ❸ Kamára tou Koráka natural arch. A perfect photo!

50 STEPS FROM HEAVEN TO THE WATERWORLD

Just 200m further on, you will come across the tiny ❹ Agíi Anárgyri Chapel. From here, steps lead down to the sea and one of the island's most popular *diving spots*. Got your snorkel? After a dip, you may be in need of some sustenance. If so, *make your way uphill on the path from the chapel, heading inland. After about 100m you will stumble on a* ❺ picnic spot with tables and benches covered by awnings.

BAREFOOT OVER WHITE SAND

As the sun rises to its peak, it's time to find a beach. *It is still 1.4km to the idyllic* ❻ Kónnos Bay. Kick back on a lounger or order yourself a drink from the *beach bar*. You've earned it. If your energy reserves are well topped up, there are plenty of opportunities to try out some water sports here. *Afterwards, walk for about 10 minutes along the tarmac road back to the main road to the* ❼ Kónnos Beach bus stop above the bay to catch the bus back.

❷ sea caves
500m 7 mins
❸ Kamára tou Koráka
200m 5 mins
❹ Agíi Anárgyri Chapel
100m 2 mins
❺ Picnic spot
1.4km 25 mins
❻ Kónnos Bay
700m 10 mins
❼ Kónnos Beach bus stop

3 A TRIP TO THE KARPAS PENINSULA

- Feed wild donkeys on rural roads
- Enjoy the golden sand of a mile-long empty beach
- Drink water with miraculous properties

Famagusta

1 day (5 hrs total driving time)

Famagusta

Distance: 235 km

HOMELY, HEAVENLY BREAKFAST

Every mile you cover heading out to the island's easternmost point will take you further away from hustle and bustle and further into incredibly beautiful scenery. It is worth setting off early from 1 Famagusta ➤ p. 117. *Follow the coastal road out to the north. After just a few miles,* pull in at 2 Melandra House ➤ p. 121, a small, private museum. Grab a coffee or – if you are there at the weekend – make sure to try their amazing breakfast.

1 Famagusta
12km 14 mins
2 Melandra House
12km 16 mins

THE MOST BEAUTIFUL LANDSCAPE AWAITS

There are three good reasons to stop at 3 Bogázi (Bogaz): a picture-perfect fishing harbour; a small stretch of beach for a refreshing swim; and excellent fish restaurants. *Once back on the road, drive through Ziyamet/Leonaríssio. Just before the next petrol station, take the road to the right in the direction of Boltasli and Dipkarpaz.* The mountains around the village of 4 Kaleburnu are as holey as Swiss cheese, with small ancient burial chambers built into their slopes. To see them, head to the Kastro Caves on the slopes to the southern end of the village. Directly opposite, you will see the 120m King's Mountain (Kral Tepesci), which not only offers amazing views from its peak but also a crystal-lined path to get there.

3 Bogázi
45km 46 mins
4 Kaleburnu
19km 17 mins

FEED WILD DONKEYS

To get to the last village on the island, you first need to *follow the road as it winds its way through some remote*

3
Geçitkale
Lefkónoiko
Akova
Gypsou
Yıldırım
Miliá
Mormenekşe
Limniá
Mutluyaka
Stylloi
Tuzla
Egkomi
Famagusta Wetlands
Sálamis
Yeni Iskele
Trikomo
Ardahan
Ardana
Kantára
Kantára
Tuzmalar
Geráni
Bahçeler
Perivólia
Boğaz
Bogázi
Büyükkonuk
Komi
Yedikonuk
Eptakómi
Ágios
Ziyam
Leonáriss
Çayırova
Ágios Theódoros
Pamuklu
Távrou
Kumyalı
Kóma tou Gia
Kólpos
Ammóchostou
1
2
3
13

FAMAGUSTA (GAZIMAĞUSA AMMÓCHOSTOS)

5 Dipkarpaz
19km 19 mins

valleys. **5 Dipkarpaz (Rizokárpaso) ➤ p. 122**, where you will end up, is an archetypal sleepy village but also a gateway to excitements beyond. From here, the real wonders of this tour will reveal themselves to you. As you head down the peninsula, do not be afraid to feed the donkeys at the edge of the road. They love bread and carrots! *Around 5km before you reach the monastery, a small road leads down to the prettiest beach on Cyprus.* **6 Golden Beach ➤ p. 123** has absolutely no facilities, making it a wonderful oasis of wilderness.

6 Golden Beach
5km 5 mins

WATER FROM A HEALING SPRING AND A TURTLE PLAYROOM

7 Apóstolos Andréas Monastery
1km 1 min

8 Sea Bird
4km 4 mins

9 Cape Andréas
31km 37 minss

Just below the **7 Apóstolos Andréas Monastery ➤ p. 123**, a stream of water emerges from the rock, which is said to have healing qualities. *A kilometre further down the tarmac road, you will reach* **8 Sea Bird** *(€)*, the easternmost restaurant on the island. Its terrace offers great sea views. From here, a sandy road will take you to **9 Cape Andréas** (Cape Victory). At the end of the cape, you will find a rock where an Aphrodite temple stood in ancient times. You can see why they built it here – the view is sensational. Ahead of you lies the eastern tip of Cyprus and the bluest of seas. To return to civilisation, you need to head back to Dipkarpaz, from where it is worth making a detour to the church of

şilköy
ónikos
Yenierenköy
(Aigiálousa)
Boltaşlı
hýlakas
Derince
Ágios Symeón
Kuruova
Koróveia
Kaleburnu
Galinóporni
Nisí Kíla
Ormos tou
Róna
Ágios Fílon
Karpaz/Karpasía
Nature Reserve
Ormos tou
Exárchou
Dipkarpaz
Rizokárpaso
South Karpaz/
Karpasía Nature Reserve
Nisí Asíro
Ormos tis
Nágkomis
Kentinari
163 m
Ammoi
Ákro Apóstolos
Andréas
Golden Beach
Ágios
Andréas
Ákro
Galounópetra
Mediterranean Sea
10 km
6.2 mi

⑩ Ágios Philon ➤ p. 122. Its ruins and the palm trees around them provide a stunning backdrop for a meal at *Oasis*, a restaurant that boasts excellent sunset views.

For one last dip in the sea, take the road to ⑪ Róna Beach and its soft sand dunes. This is one of the beaches where turtles construct their nests between June and September. *Just before you get to Gialousa/ Yenierenköy*, make a stop at ⑫ Ágios Thýrsos chapel ➤ p. 122. Head down the steps here to discover the chapel in a cave and an undergound spring. Once back in ⑬ Bogázi, it will be time for something to eat. And it is hard to beat the romanticism of a meal on the quay under the stars before tackling the last stretch of the journey back to ① Famagusta.

⑩ Ágios Philon
10km 10 mins
⑪ Róna Beach
8km 8 mins
⑫ Ágios Thýrsos
44km 44 mins
⑬ Bogázi
23km 23 mins
① Famagusta

Cape Andréas is at the easternmost tip of Cyprus: all you can see from here is the sea

GOOD TO KNOW

HOLIDAY BASICS

ARRIVAL

GETTING THERE

The flight time from the UK to Cyprus is approx. 4–5 hours. For trips of up to 90 days, UK (and US) visitors do not require a visa. However, your passport must be valid for at least three months after you plan to leave Cyprus. You can also enter Cyprus via Turkey, but this takes considerably longer. The easiest and cheapest way to get away from the airport to the south as quickly as possible is to get an Airport Shuttle bus into town (9 euros). Buses to other towns cost between 4 and 9 euros. There are shuttle buses available at all airports but they are not equally reliable (some, for example, don't operate at night).

INSIDER TIP
Get me to the beach

+ 2 hours time difference

Cyprus is two hours ahead of the UK all year round.

Adaptor Type G

Cyprus uses the same Type G plugs as the UK. Adaptors are readily available for visitors from other countries.

CLIMATE & WHEN TO GO

Cyprus is lucky enough to get more than 300 sunny days per year. In the summer, it gets extremely hot but as long as you are within easy reach of the beach, you won't care! If you want

Hanging out in Pafós

to travel around the island, the best time to do so is spring (from March to May) when the trees are in blossom. Sea temperatures remain pleasant enough to swim well into November

RESPONSIBLE TRAVEL
It doesn't take a lot to be environmentally friendly while travelling. Don't just think about your carbon footprint when flying to and from your holiday destination, but also about how you can protect nature and culture abroad. As a tourist it is especially important to respect the environment, look out for local products, cycle instead of drive, save water and much more. If you would like to find out more about eco-tourism, please visit *ecotourism.org*.

GETTING AROUND

BORDER CROSSINGS

At the time of writing, there are nine checkpoints on the north-south border – the Green Line. Your ID will be scanned at the checkpoints. You can take goods for personal use with a value of up to 260 euros across the border in both directions; customs officials do perform random checks. Bringing counterfeit branded goods into the south from the north is strictly prohibited – you risk confiscation if you do. If entering the south from the north, you can bring a maximum of two packs of cigarettes with you.

BUS

Buses connect all the towns and cities within the relevant part of the island.

From these urban hubs, buses go to the villages in the region. Day tickets cost 5 euros for each region (very long cross-country trips can be covered under this tariff). Intercity buses tend to be quicker but you pay for this (7–17 euros for a return ticket). There is a comprehensive list of routes, timetables and prices at *cyprusbybus.com*.

TAXI

Shared taxis, which pick you up from a pre-arranged location and can cover the same long distances as the buses, vary wildly in price (8–35 euros). More info is available at *travelexpress.com.cy*. These taxis are available in both parts of Cyprus but in the north (where they are called *dolmuş*) there is unfortunately no good website offering information. Instead, you will need to go to a tourist information office if you want to find out more about this option.

In a normal taxi in the south, you pay 0.953 euros/km in the daytime and 1.10 euros/km at night. This is on top of a pick-up fee of 3.80 euros in the day and 4.80 euros at night. Make sure your taxi driver turns on the meter.

VEHICLE HIRE

Depending on the season, a small car costs between 35 and 35 euros per day. If you want to cross the border in your car, make sure you inform the car-hire company. You will need to purchase extra insurance (at the checkpoints) at 20 euros for up to three days, or 30 euros for a whole month.

The speed limit on Cyprus's fastest roads is 100kph. On country roads, it is 80kph, and in villages, towns and cities it is 50kph. In the north, your blood alcohol level must be at zero when driving. The south allows you a slightly higher limit of 0.5 per mille (this is stricter than the UK). Using your phone and smoking at the wheel are strictly prohibited across the island.

For Brits, driving in Cyprus is relatively easy since the islanders drive on the left.

EMERGENCIES

CONSULATES & EMBASSIES

British High Commission

Alexander Pallis Street (PO Box 21978) | 1587 Nicosia | tel. 357 22 861100 | ukincyprus.fco.gov.uk/en

Irish Embassy

7 Aiantas Street (PO Box 23848) | Nicosia | tel. 357 22 818183 | dfa.ie/irish-embassy/cyprus

US Embassy

Metochiou & Ploutarchou Street | 2407 Engomi | Nicosia | tel. 357 22 393939 | cy.usembassy.gov

Canadian Embassy (GREECE)

48 Eth. Anistaseos | 15231 Athens | Greece | tel. 21 07 27 34 00 / canadainternational.gc.ca/greece-grece

HEALTH

The health services on Cyprus are good and many doctors speak English.

EMERGENCY SERVICES

Southern Cyprus: call 199 or 112 for police, fire brigade and ambulance.

FESTIVALS & EVENTS

ALL YEAR ROUND

FEBRUARY
Carnival (Limassol): the parties and parades (photo) attract thousands of visitors. *limassolmunicipal.com.cy/carnival*

EASTER
Bonfires, parades, games and processions all over the island

APRIL
Street Life Festival *(FB: streetlifefest)*

MAY/JUNE
Rose Festival (Agrós)
Eco Day (Kómi Kebir/Büyükkonuk): sustainable village fete
Feast of Kataklysmos (Lárnaka, Agía Nápa, Limassol): Festival of Noah's Flood, with markets and games in, on, by and with water.
International Bellapaís Music Festival (Kerýneia/Girne): classical music
Güzelyourt Orange Festival: parade, events and tastings

JULY
Festival of Ancient Greek Drama (ancient theatres of Nicosia, Koúrion and Páfos). *greekdramafest.com*

AUGUST/SEPTEMBER
Fengaros (Kato Drys): rock/pop/folk
Lefkara Summer Festival: traditional crafts and entertainment
Wine Festival (Limassol): *limassolmunicipal.com.cy/en/wine-festival*
Pomegranate Festival (Omidia): fruit folklore and more
Grape festivals (wine-producing villages such as Vása, Lófou and Arsos)

OCTOBER
Medieval Festival (Agía Nápa)
Eco Day (Kómi Kebir/Büyükkonuk): sustainable village fete

NOVEMBER
Zivania Festival (Alona, Peléndri): performances and tastings

Northern Cyprus: call 155 for police. Call 112 for ambulance. Call 199 for fire brigade.

ESSENTIALS

BEACHES

In southern Cyprus, there are 74 Blue Flag beaches (the internationally recognised system for clean beaches). In the south, all beaches are publicly accessible and do not charge entry fees. Many beaches in the north are privately owned or leased and charge entry.

CAMPING

There are only a few very basic campsites in both parts of the island and they are mostly on the coast or in the Tróodos mountains. Some glamping locations are starting to emerge to compete with the more basic sites.

CUSTOMS

For non-EU countries, there are limits on what goods you can bring and out of the country. It is worth checking these limits in advance, but at the moment 200 cigarettes and 1 litre of spirits is the maximum if you are flying in and out of the UK.

HIKING

Cyprus is a great place, to walk but make sure you always have a sunhat and a bottle of water with you. Rocky paths, thorns and snakes also mean that decent walking shoes and long trousers are a must.

MONEY

There are two different currencies in use on the island. In the south, people use the euro, and in the north, the Turkish lira. Exchange rates are impossible to predict as they can vary enormously.

HOW MUCH DOES IT COST?

Taxi	0.95/1.20 euros *per km (day/night)*
Coffee	2.50 euros *for a cup*
Deck chair	2.50 euros/day
Wine	from 15 euros *for a bottle in a restaurant*
Petrol	around 1.37 euros *for 1 litre super unleaded*
Kebab	4–6 euros *for a kebab in a flatbread*

TURKISH CYPRIOT NATIONAL HOLIDAYS

1 Jan	New Year
23 April	Children's Day
April or May	Şeker Bayramı (end of Ramadan)
1 May	Labour Day
19 May	Day of Youth and Sports
late June or early July	Kurban Bayramı (Sacrifice Festival)
20 July	Day of Turkish Intervention
30 Aug	Victory Day
29 Oct	Foundation of the Turkish Republic
15 Nov	Day of the Proclamation of the Turkish Republic of Northern Cyprus

GREEK CYPRIOT NATIONAL HOLIDAYS

1 Jan	New Year
6 Jan	Epiphany
Feb or March	Green Monday (start of Lent)
25 March	Greek Independence Day
1 April	Cypriot National Day
April or May	Orthodox Good Friday
April or May	Orthodox Easter Monday
1 May	Labour Day
June	Whit Monday
15 Aug	Assumption
1 Oct	Independence Day
28 Oct	Ochi Day
25/26 Dec	Christmas

NUDISM

Nudism is prohibited across the island and topless sunbathing is only allowed in the south.

PHOTOGRAPHY

Taking photos of anything related to the military is strictly forbidden. This includes the border and checkpoints.

POST

Stamps are available from post offices, which are mostly open Monday–Friday 8am–3pm.

TELEPHONE

The international dialling code for southern Cyprus is 00357. In the north, use the Turkish dialling code 0090 and then add 392 for landline numbers or 533/542 for mobiles.

TIPPING

A service fee is nearly always included on the bill. However, it is not uncommon to top this up by around 10%. Leave the tip on the table when you go.

WEATHER

High season
Low season

	JAN	FEB	MAR	APR	MAY	JUN	JUL	AUG	SEP	OCT	NOV	DEC
Daytime temperatures (°C)	15°	15°	19°	24°	29°	33°	38°	38°	33°	28°	23°	17°
Night-time temperatures (°C)	5°	5°	7°	10°	14°	18°	21°	21°	18°	14°	11°	7°
Sunshine hours/day	5	6	7	8	10	12	12	12	10	8	6	5
Rainy days/month	11	9	5	3	3	1	0	0	1	3	5	9
Sea temperatures in °C	16°	16°	17°	18°	20°	21°	23°	24°	25°	24°	21°	18°

Sunshine hours/day · Rainy days/month · Sea temperatures in °C

USEFUL WORDS
GREEK

SMALLTALK

Yes/no/maybe	ne/'ochi/'issos	Ναι/ Όχι/Ισως
Please/Thank you	paraka'lo/efcharis'to	Παρακαλώ/ Ευχαριστώ
Good morning/good evening/goodnight!	kalli'mera/kalli'spera/ kalli'nichta!	Καληέραμ/ Καλησπέρα!/ Καληνύχτα!
Hello/ goodbye (formal)/ goodbye (informal)!	'ya (su/sass)/ a'dio/ ya (su/sass)!	Γεία (σου/σας)!/ αντίο!/Γεία (σου/ σας)!
My name is …	me 'lene …	Με λένεÖ …
What's your name?	poss sass 'lene?	Πως σας λένε?
Excuse me/sorry	me sig'chorite/ sig'nomi	Με συγχωρείτε / Συγνώημ
Pardon?	o'riste?	Ορίστε?
I (don't) like this	Af'to (dhen) mu a'ressi	Αυτό (δεν) ουμ αρέσει

SYMBOLS

ATM
P
TAXI

EATING & DRINKING

Could you please book a table for tonight for four?	Klis'te mass parakal'lo 'enna tra'pezi ya a'popse ya 'tessera 'atoma	Κλείστε ασμ παρακαλώ ένα τραπέζι γιά απόψε γιά τέσσερα άτοαμ
The menu, please	tonn ka'taloggo parakal'lo	Τον κατάλογο παρακαλώ
Could I please have ... ?	tha 'ithella na 'echo ...?	Θα ήθελα να έχο ...?
more/less	pjo/li'gotäre	ρπιό/λιγότερο
with/without ice/ sparkling	me/cho'ris 'pa-go/ anthrakik'ko	εμ/χωρίς πάγο/ ανθρακικό
(un)safe drinking water	(mi) 'possimo nä'ro	(μη) Πόσιμο νερό
vegetarian/allergy	chorto'fagos/allerg'ia	Χορτοφάγος/ Αλλεργία
May I have the bill, please?	'thel'lo na pli'rosso parakal'lo	Θέλω να πληρώσω παρακαλώ

MISCELLANEOUS

Where is ...?	pu tha vro ...?	Που θα βρω ...?
What time is it?	Ti 'ora 'ine?	Τι ώρα είναι?
How much does... cost ?	Posso 'kani ...?	Πόσο κάνει ...?
Where can I find internet access?	pu bor'ro na vro 'prosvassi sto índernett?	Που πορώμ να βρω πρόσβαση στο ίντερνετ?
pharmacy/ chemist	farma'kio/ ka'tastima	Φαρακείομ/ Κατάστηαμ καλλυντικών
fever/pain /diarrhoea/ nausea	piret'tos/'ponnos/ dhi'arria/ana'gula	Πυρετός/Πόνος/ Διάρροια/Αναγούλα
Help!/Watch out! Be Careful	Wo'ithia!/Prosso'chi!/ Prosso'chi!	Βοήθεια!/Προσοχή!/ Προσοχή!
Forbidden/banned	apa'gorăfsi/ apago'räwäte	Απαγόρευση/ απαγορέυεται
0/1/2/3/4/5/6/7/8/9/ 10/100/1000	mi'dhen / 'enna / 'dhio / 'tria / 'tessera / 'pende / 'eksi / ef'ta / och'to / e'nea / dhekka / eka'to / 'chilia / 'dhekka chil'iades	ηδένμ/ένα/δύο/τρία/ τέσσερα/πέντε/έξι/ εφτά/οχτώ/ εννέα/ δέκα/εκατό/χίλια/ δέκα χιλιάδες

USEFUL WORDS
TURKISH

SMALLTALK

Yes/no/maybe	Evet/hayır/belki
Please/thank you	Lütfen./Teşekkür (ederim) *or* Mersi
Good morning/afternoon/evening/ night	Günaydın!/İyi Günler!/İyi Akşamlar!/İyi Geceler!
Hello/Goodbye	Merhaba!/Allaha ısmarladık!
Bye	Hoşçakal (Plural: Hoşçakalın)/Bye bye!
My name is ...	Adım ... *or* İsmim ...
What's your name (formal)?	Sizin adınız ne?/Sizin isminiz ne?
What's your name (informal)?	Senin adın ne?/Senin ismin ne?
I am from ...	... den/dan geliyorum.
sorry/excuse me	Afedersin!/Afedersiniz!
I (don't) like this	Beğendim./Beğenmedim.
I would like.../Do you have...?	... istiyorum/... var mı?

SYMBOLS

ATM
P
TAXI

EATING & DRINKING

Could I have the menu please?	**Menü lütfen.**
Could I please have …?	**... alabilir miyim lütfen?**
bottle/carafe/glass	**şişe/karaf/bardak**
knife/fork/spoon	**bıçak/çatal/kaşık**
salt/pepper/sugar	**tuz/karabiber/şeker**
vinegar/oil	**sirke/zeytinyağı**
milk/cream/lemon	**süt/kaymak/limon**
fizzy/still water	**karbonatlı/karbonatsız**
vegetarian/ allergy	**vejetaryan/alerji**
Could I have the bill please?	**Hesap lütfen.**
bill/receipt/tip	**fatura/fiş/bahşiş**
cash/debit card/credit card	**nakit/banka kartı/kredi kartı**

MISCELLANEOUS

Where is/are…?	**Nerede ...?/neredeler ...?**
today/tomorrow/yesterday	**bugün/yarın/dün**
How much is …?	**... ne kadar? Fiyatı ne?**
Where I can I get internet access?	**İnternete nereden girebilirim?**
Help!/Watch out!	**İmdat!/Dikkat!**
pharmacy/drugstore	**eczane/ıtriyat mağazası**
broken/doesn't work	**bozuk/çalışmıyor**
fever (temperature)/pain/diarrhoea/ nausea	**ateş/ağrı/ishal/bulantı**
(non-)drinking water	**içme suyu (değil)**
open/closed	**açık/kapalı**
entrance	**giriş/garaj kapısı**
exit	**çıkış/garaj çıkışı**
toilets/women/men	**tuvalet (WC)/bayan/bay**
Sorry, I did not understand that	**Özür dilerim, anlamadım**
I would like to hire a car	**bir otomobil/araba kiralamak istiyorum.**
bank/cash machine	**banka/ATM**
supermarket	**süpermarket**
bakery/market	**fırın/pazar**
0/1/2/3/4/5/6/7/8/9/ 10/100/1000	**sıfır/bir/iki/üç/dört/beş/altı/yedi/ sekiz/dokuz/on/yüz/bin**

HOLIDAY VIBES

FOR RELAXATION & CHILLING

FOR BOOKWORMS & FILM BUFFS

APHRODITE – THE NAKED TRUTH

Hello, hello! The whole (erotic) truth about the ancient cult around Aphrodite in graphic novel form. Not for kids.

BITTER LEMONS

Lawrence Durrell's poetic account of the time he spent on Cyprus in the 1950s. It was a time when donkeys still roamed the streets, and British colonial troops clashed with freedom fighters around the island. (First published 1957.)

STORY OF THE GREEN LINE

Walls divide. Kypros and Murat are guards on either side of the border. In their day jobs, they could be required to shoot at each other but in reality they share a common history. (2017, Director: Panicos Chrysanthou)

SMUGGLING HENDRIX

This charming film tells the story of what happens when a dog roams around, illegally crosses a border between two enemy sides and leaves EU territory. (2018, Director: Marios Piperides)

PLAYLIST

0:58

MINUS ONE – ALTER EGO
Home-made rock which made it all the way to Eurovision.

TÁLTSIE – HOLDING STONES
A young indie and soul singer with a unique sound who writes and performs her own songs.

MONSIEUR DOUMANI – PISSOÚRIN
Excellent Cyprus folk trio.

ANDREAS RODOSTHENOUS – BLUES FOR NIKI
Jazz, which oscillates between classical and experimental

ANNA VISSI – KANENAS
Cyprus's most famous pop singer. Three times a contestant for Eurovision.

RÜYA TANER – PERCUSSION COLORS
Renowned concert pianist.

*Find your holiday soundtrack on **Spotify** under **MARCO POLO** Cyprus*

Or scan this code with the Spotify app

ONLINE

APHRODITE'S KITCHEN
Christina Loucas is not just a great cook, she also knows how to photograph food properly. The recipes in her blog blend the food of her childhood with that of her new home (Canada) (afroditeskitchen.com).

CYPRIOT & PROUD
Blog or app: Locals' tips for everything the island has to offer, from food to hotels and partying.

GEORGIOU'S WORLD
Georgiou is a Brit of Cypriot heritage who enjoys poking fun at both of his national identities in short YouTube clips.

NTAXI
Cyprus's version of Uber. The practical alternative to marked taxis

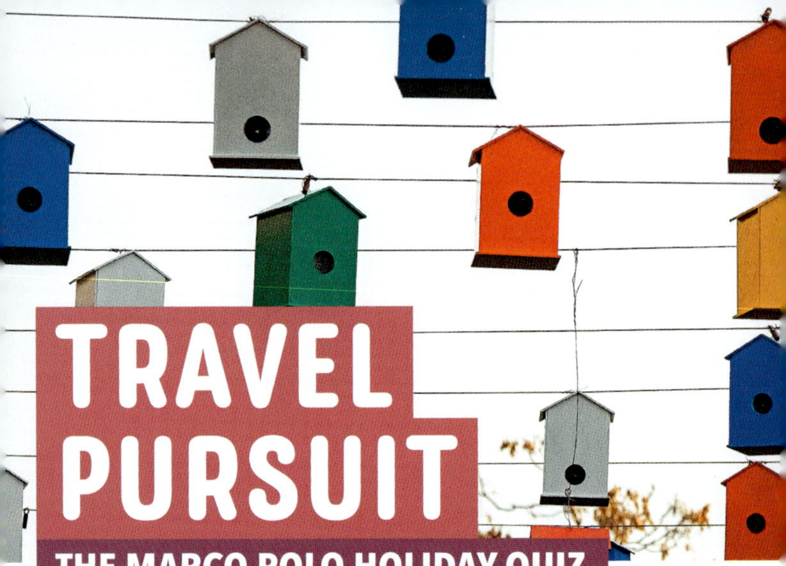

TRAVEL PURSUIT

THE MARCO POLO HOLIDAY QUIZ

Have you worked out what makes Cyprus tick? Use this quiz to test your knowledge of the island's customs and idiosyncracies. The answers are at the bottom of the page with further information on pages 18–23.

❶ Whose bites do you most want to avoid on the island?
a) The Levant viper
b) British teenagers trying to show their "love"
c) The carnival vampire

❷ How heavy is a fully grown Cypriot watermelon?
a) 25kg
b) 15kg
c) 5kg

❸ Which traditional Cypriot pastime causes uproar among activists across Europe?
a) Trapping birds
b) Easter bonfires
c) Hunting season

❹ Why do some people call the city in southern Cyprus "Limassolgrad"?
a) Because it is always two degrees cooler there
b) Because so many Russians live there
c) Because the products made there are of such high quality

❺ Why is the dividing line between north and south Cyprus called the Green Line?
a) Because there is so much greenery
b) Because it was originally drawn on a map with a green pen
c) Because green is the colour of reunification

Correct answers: 1a, 2b, 3a, 4b, 5b, 6c, 7b, 8a, 9a, 10c

6 How many guests would the hosts expect at a traditional Cypriot wedding?

a) 50 people
b) 700 people
c) 2,000 people

7 Which Cypriot town has three names?

a) Agía Nápa
b) Famagusta
c) Pólis

8 What is the common name for the salt that was once harvested in Lárnaka?

a) White gold
b) The snow of seasoning
c) Mysterious white powder

9 What is the most popular girls' name among Greek Cypriots?

a) Maria
b) Aphrodite
c) Eleni

10 What addition was made to St Sophia's cathedral?

a) A satellite dish
b) A weather vane
c) A minaret

INDEX

WE WANT TO HEAR FROM YOU!

Did you have a great holiday? Is there something on your mind? Whatever it is, let us know! Whether you want to praise the guide, alert us to errors or give us a personal tip – MARCO POLO would be pleased to hear from you. Please contact us by email

We do everything we can to provide the very latest information for your trip. Nevertheless, despite all of our authors' thorough research, errors can creep in. MARCO POLO does not accept any liability for this.

e-mail: sales@heartwoodpublishing.co.uk

Credits
Cover Picture: Rocky coast at Cape Gréko near Agía Nápa (Schapowalow: R. Schmid)
Photos: CIPS: M. Gittis (9, 107); DuMont Bildarchiv: Richter (11, 26/27); huber images: J. Huber (outer front flap, inner front flap), 1, 6/7), R. Schmid (4/5, 38/39, 42, 77, 85, 89, 112/113, 117), R. Spila (80/81, 124/125), R. Taylor (123); Laif: F. Barbagallo (73), J. - P. Böning (132/133), M. Gumm (54/55), J. - P. Boening (96/97); Laif/hemis.fr: L. Maisant (104); mauritius images /Alamy/Alamy Stock Photos/Imageimage (28); mauritius images: S. Beuthan (70); mauritius images// Alamy/Zoonar GmbH (12/13); mauritius images/ Alamy: E. Fesenko (49), Findlay (45), C. Hanninen (64/65), A. Hasson (30/31, 115), I. Henley (20), A. King (8, 32/33), H. Kotowski (131), H. Milas (52, 69), I. Rutherford (103, 142/143, 144), R. Wyatt (108/109); mauritius images/Alamy/Alamy Stock Photos: A. Kucherova (10), I. Rutherford (19), J. Windsor (135); mauritius images/Alamy/Bildagentur-online: Joko (74); mauritius images/Alamy/eFesenko (95); mauritius images/Alamy/Iwebbtravel (back cover flap); mauritius images/Alamy/iWebbtravel (51); mauritius images/Alamy/LatitudeStock (92); mauritius images/ Alamy/PhotoStock-Israel(87); mauritius images/Cavan Images: J. Langley (114, 119); mauritius images/ imagebroker: S. Auth (126); mauritius images/image-BROKER: C. Handl (22), A. Isachenk (24/25); mauritius images/Imagebroker: N. Probst (35); mauritius images/Imagebroker/STELLA (60); mauritius images/ Imagebroker/White Star: M. Gumm (62, 79); mauritius images/robertharding: M. Runkel (121); picture-alliance/ZB (101); T. Stankiewicz (14/15); C. Sternberg (147); T. P. Widmann (27, 46, 91)

5th Edition – fully revised and updated 2024
Worldwide Distribution: Heartwood Publishing Ltd, Bath, United Kingdom
www.heartwoodpublishing.co.uk

Authors: Christiane Sternberg
Editor: Christina Sothmann
Picture editor: Gabriele Forst
Cartography: © MAIRDUMONT, Ostfildern (pp. 36–37, 126, 128, 130–31, outer flap, pull-out map)
© MAIRDUMONT, Ostfildern, using data from OpenStreetMap, Licence CC-BY-SA 2.0 (pp. 40–41, 48, 56–57, 59, 66–67, 78, 82–83, 86, 98–99, 110–111).
Cover design and pull-out map design: bilekjaeger _Kreativagentur with Zukunftswerkstatt, Stuttgart
Page design: Langenstein Communication GmbH, Ludwigsburg

Heartwood Publishing credits:
Translated from the German by John Owen, Kathleen Becker, Jennifer Walcoff Neuheiser, Suzanne Kirkbright
Editors: Felicity Laughton, Kate Michell, Sophie Blacksell Jones, Rosamund Sales
Prepress: Summerlane Books, Bath
Printed in India

MARCO POLO AUTHOR
CHRISTIANE STERNBERG
This author knows all the island's secrets. After living in Cyprus for 15 years, she has developed a feeling for where scenic beauty lies hidden or where new trends are emerging. Her friends on both sides of the dividing line constantly provide her with the best insider tips. And, Christiane is particularly happy that sustainable tourism is now gaining ground in people's minds and in villages!

DOS & DON'TS

HOW TO AVOID SLIP-UPS & BLUNDERS

DO BE AWARE OF FAKES

If you find high-fashion items for sale at very low prices in Northern Cyprus, beware. And don't show them off to customs' officers as they are probably fakes and they may be confiscated.

DON'T ASK A WOMAN'S AGE

In Cyprus, it is considered exceptionally rude to ask a woman hold old she is. It is even very rare for newspapers to mention the age of people in their articles.

DON'T DISCUSS CONSPIRACY THEORIES

Cypriots love a conspiracy theory, and you're better off not getting involved. It is commonly believed on Cyprus that the CIA is responsible for the island's division. If you get confronted with a "truth", the best idea is to nod along and change the subject as soon as possible.

DON'T TRY AND PAY SEPARATELY

Who is going to pick up the bill? In Cyprus, it is considered a point of politeness for one person to pay a bill in full so don't start getting your calculators out while the waiter is at your table.

DON'T MENTION THE NORTH

For Greek Cypriots Northern Cyprus is an occupied territory. End of. Very few of them have been there and they often struggle to understand why tourists would want to support the "illegal regime" with their money. As a result, be careful about bringing up the subject of Northern Cyprus's undoubted beauty when in polite southern company.